REDEFINING
✓POSSIBLE

REDEFINING
POSSIBLE

Proven Strategies *to*
Break Belief Barriers *and*
Create Your New Normal

RON ALFORD *and* DUSTIN HILLIS

SouthwesternBooks

Redefining Possible: Proven Strategies to Break Belief Barriers and Create Your New Normal was published by Southwestern Books. Southwestern Books is an imprint of Southwestern Publishing House, Inc., 2451 Atrium Way, Nashville, TN 37214. Southwestern Publishing House is a wholly owned subsidiary of Southwestern Family of Companies, Inc., Nashville, TN.

swpublishinghouse.com | 800-358-0560

Published in association with Southwestern Consulting.
info@southwesternconsulting.com
southwesternconsulting.com | 615-391-2834

Southwestern Books are available at special quantity discounts for bulk purchases for sales promotions, premiums, fundraising, or educational use. Special books or book excerpts can be created to fit specific needs at the compliance of the author/s. For details, write sales@southwesternbooks.com.

To learn how to bring the inspiring message of *Redefining Possible* to your next event, contact info@southwesternspeakers.com.

Cover design by Kristen Ingebretson
Interior design by Vicky Shea

Scripture is taken from the Holy Bible, New Living Translation, copyright © 1996, 2004, 2015 by Tyndale House Foundation. Used by permission of Tyndale House Publishers, Inc., Carol Stream, IL 60188. All rights reserved.

ISBN: 978-1-941800-50-8 – Hardcover
978-1-941800-52-2 – Softcover
979-8-200797-27-1 – Audiobook
Library of Congress Control Number: 2020909374

Printed in the United States of America
10 9 8 7 6 5 4 3 2

Dedication

From Dustin: I dedicate this book (and everything I do) first to God: my identity is in Christ alone. Second, to my beautiful wife, Kyah: after being married for fifteen years, I find myself loving you more and more every day. I love you. Third, to my daughter, Haven—my little entrepreneur and sweetheart: you are a gift from God, and you always brighten my day. Fourth, to my Southwestern family: thank you for all that you do every day to invest in people and inspire them to impact the world in a positive way!

From Ron: I'd like to dedicate this book to my three kids, Van, P. K., and Hartley, and to my wife, Desireé. This book gives so much purpose to every challenge our family has faced and will face in the future, and it makes all the joys that much sweeter. You four are my biggest inspirations for all that I do. I am driven to be the best example that a man can be, to use every gift that God has given me, and to be someone who you four are proud to call "Dad" and "Husband." I hope this book honors you and shows how much I love you as well as how grateful I am to God for all He has given us.

From Dustin and Ron: This book is dedicated to everyone who is out there searching. We believe that God put us all on the planet for a reason. Sadly, some people go their whole lives without finding their purpose. In fact, massive numbers of people know they could be getting more out of life but don't know how. This book is dedicated to those who are willing to look into the mirror and admit that they want to make changes . . . and not let where they have been hold them back. If this describes you, we invite you to read this book and redefine possible.

Contents

Foreword

Perhaps the greatest benefit of working so long with a company that attracts uniquely motivated young people, and then gives them a chance to either fall flat on their face or fly to the moon, is seeing some of them rise beyond the common and selfish quest for personal achievement and center on a mission of making the world better. Dustin Hillis and Ron Alford have done just that, making a great and progressive impact on that mission by giving us *Redefining Possible*.

As president of Southwestern Advantage, I have known each of these young men since they were college students selling educational systems door-to-door in our award-winning internship program. I consider it a personal privilege to have seen Dustin and Ron develop into record setters and catalysts in the success of so many others. I have seen them with their families. I have seen them at work and at play. I have seen them strive every day to live consistently well and positively impact the world. They go about this not in a way where they get everything right every time (no one does that), but in a way that is based on a complete lack of vanity and an immense sense of gratitude for their opportunities and abilities.

Dustin and Ron have achieved great levels of professional success, yet they write from positions of deep humility. They fearlessly reveal some of their most profound personal failures, fully accepting responsibility—and therefore, speaking from places where we all can connect.

This is far from a self-help book. It's a *self-realization* book. The seven strategies outlined here have three things in common: they are rooted in reality, they work (if we do), and they challenge us to be better at life.

As I read this book, I was expecting it to be "good," with useful information. I wasn't expecting it to get under my skin. With its powerful formula, this book can help literally anyone reach a new awareness of what they can accomplish and, more important, *why* they should strive to redefine possible.

There are books about focus, and there are books about taking ownership. Yet in a lightbulb moment, Ron and Dustin have combined these strategies powerfully to create a lifelong, sustainable vision to accomplish more and live with greater purpose. This in turn creates a unique and comprehensive synergy of forces and abilities.

There are also books about increasing belief and gaining more confidence. Yet in combining those two with faith as the result, the authors have caused me to think differently about faith in my daily pursuits (apart from any religious connotations). The book then pours the accelerant called impact on these potent fuel sources, igniting them and pulling everything together.

Most significant to me personally is the concept in chapter 5 called "confidence anchors." All people have wins, and all people have losses. Too often, we dwell repeatedly on our losses, and we tend to put less emphasis on our wins. As Dustin and Ron say, "We experience storms all day, every day. That's why we need anchors." A confidence anchor is "a victory that you can revisit—a memory of a time when you redefined what was possible." Everyone has had at least one of those times. By nurturing that memory, we can create a stepping-stone to another moment of redefinition. The authors wisely admonish us to avoid complacency in this process, because "as soon as you've peaked, everything else is downhill."

The lessons in this book have been vitally important to Southwestern Advantage, the business within Southwestern Family of Companies that I am most involved in. We have had to redefine our entire business model due to the global COVID-19 health crisis. For a century and a half, our business had been based on selling educational systems door-to-door. With municipalities, states, and even countries in various stages of lockdown, we realized that going door-to-door was clearly not going to be possible in the same way it had been previously.

Ron and Dustin have been frequent speakers and coaches to the team members and independent educational system dealers at Southwestern Advantage. Their underlying message—that "possible" is up to us—has helped us to fuel our own redefinition at Southwestern Advantage. Our dedicated team has employed every one of the seven strategies in this book, and we are succeeding in redefining possible.

Dustin Hillis and Ron Alford have spent three years working

on this book. They could not have known the book would be coming out to all of us during what will one day be called our world's COVID-19 "moment." Much of what was familiar, in work and in play, has been shuttered and made inaccessible due to the advance of a microscopic and unfeeling virus. Sinking into a sense of despair and hopelessness could be a daily excuse. That's why this book is so important—why this is a book for our times. When the hope-poisoning word *impossible* can easily become a collective mindset, a potent antidote must be readily at hand.

Redefining Possible is that antidote.

Dan Moore
President, Southwestern Advantage
September 2020

The Power of Possible

It was March 2020, and Southwestern Consulting was on the precipice of reaching a new high. As one of the world's fastest-growing sales and leadership coaching, keynote speaking, and consulting organizations, the company had earned $17 million in revenue the previous year and was looking to hit the $20 million mark in 2020. Around the world, more than one hundred certified coaches were growing their business and achieving their goals. All signs pointed toward even more explosive growth in the year to come . . . and we, the authors, Dustin Hillis and Ron Alford, were helping to lead the way.

Then, faster than anyone could have imagined, everything changed with the COVID-19 pandemic and the global state of emergency. The whole world was thrown into chaos. In the following weeks, US governors ordered citizens to shelter in place. Universities across the country sent their students home before spring break—for good. Parents had to oversee their kids' learning, now exclusively at home. Employees grabbed their laptop and set up an office in their spare bedroom or at the dining room table.

Suddenly, everything became virtual.

For our leadership team at Southwestern Consulting, this shift presented an enormous challenge. Like everyone else in the early months of the pandemic, we (Dustin and Ron) found ourselves facing circumstances completely out of our control. Our business model had been created for us to meet with our clients in person, conduct workshops in offices, give speeches to full rooms, and fly across the country to shadow and support our team members in their home offices. New coaches flew to our corporate offices in Nashville to spend time with the team as well as to receive intensive training. In addition to one-on-one coaching work, Southwestern Consulting had planned more than ten events in April, May, and June, and members of our leadership team were traveling up to three times a week. In March, however, we experienced an 80 percent cancellation rate in workshops. Clients started calling to put payments on hold. And team members began to question how they could do their jobs.

2020 forced us to redefine possible—and fast.

Fortunately, one thing that we knew the pandemic couldn't take from us was our mindset and how we chose to respond to these uncontrollable forces. We were already operating from a positive framework, using the seven foundational strategies you are about to learn in this book. As company leaders, we also deployed a specific tool Dustin created called the RAFT™ technique, which we use with our coaching clients during times of crisis. We found it helpful to apply this technique during the state of emergency:

R: Realize an event is happening to you.

A: Accept that the event is occurring.

F: Focus on what you can control.

T: Transform the negative event into positive momentum.

For us, using RAFT in March 2020 looked like this: We **realized** that the COVID-19 crisis was happening. We quickly **accepted** our circumstances and **focused** on what we could control. And we **transformed** the negative event into positive momentum. (You'll read more about RAFT in Appendix A of this book.)

We met with the senior partners at Southwestern Consulting when the crisis began, focusing on health and safety, but we balanced our actions by making sure not to overreact. We reminded our team members that even though the circumstances seemed unpredictable, there were some things they *could* control, including their own attitudes and schedules. We encouraged everyone to take ownership of the situation, recognizing that we were all working from home, in a pandemic, and the results would be up to us. We also believed in our mission and had faith that we would succeed.

As a company, we came up with a game plan, arranging video calls, ramping up our communication, keeping our team's health and safety front of mind, and ultimately focusing on our mission of impact. Most significantly, we pivoted all of our workshops to an online model, which was a huge success. By the end of April 2020, our coaches had booked more workshops than they had in April 2019.

Like you, we had grand plans for what we were going to accomplish in 2020. Despite COVID-19 throwing a wrench in our lives, we utilized the RAFT technique to help center ourselves in the chaos, working to redefine possible—both individually and as a business. Now, Southwestern Consulting is breaking records in recruiting and selling . . . all thanks to the tools in this book.

LET'S GET STARTED

How did we get here? We certainly don't have it all figured out. But ask anyone who has known us for a long time, and they will agree: we are not the same people we were five or ten years ago.

We are writing this book because we believe we were put on this earth to learn and share. We've each been given more than we deserve, and we are truly grateful for God's goodness and grace in our lives. We appreciate both the mountaintops and the valleys in our respective journeys. Each of us has hit rock bottom and crawled our way back out of the pit of despair—more than once.

We are not only coauthors but also longtime colleagues, associates, and friends. Before finding Southwestern, we had very little real-world business experience. Our careers are intimately tied to Southwestern Family of Companies, a diverse group of organizations (including Southwestern Consulting) that spans the world and encompasses a range of industries, including leadership training and consulting, sales and leadership coaching, publishing, executive search services, direct sales, investment advising, real estate, insurance, travel, and school fundraising. Since 1855, Southwestern Family of Companies has been committed to building purpose-driven people, and today, those people are inspired to build principle-guided businesses that impact the world.

The principles we're about to share with you in this book are rooted in the mission and proven strategies developed by Southwestern Family of Companies. Many of these techniques and strategies come from decades of successful training within Southwestern's various organizations. As longtime employees and company leaders, we have worked hard to hone and expand upon these time-honored concepts, applying them diligently to our own professional and personal lives. These strategies have made an incredible impact—not only in our own lives but also in the lives of the countless people we help and coach.

For the two of us, this content is deeply personal, so at times the book's narrative will switch back and forth as we talk about how certain events in our lives have helped us to redefine possible. Most of the book, however, is written in our collective voice—and that's because we are both passionately committed to the strategies and techniques you are about to learn.

Before we get started, we'd like to officially introduce one another.

From Dustin

These principles have reaped massive results in my friend Ron's life.

Ron Alford is the third-highest lifetime producer at Southwestern Advantage, a sales and leadership program that was founded in 1868 for university students and is part of Southwestern Family of

Companies. After twenty years with Southwestern Advantage, Ron joined Southwestern Consulting in 2013. He continues to break records as the top producer at Southwestern Consulting, where he earned a senior partnership in record time. Ron is now the vice president of recruiting at Southwestern Coaching, the sales and leadership, one-on-one coaching arm of Southwestern Consulting. He is one of only two recipients of the Trifecta Award, the highest honor at Southwestern Coaching. This award is given to those who reach the peak of selling, recruiting, and team leadership.

Ron is also an avid endurance runner, having completed many ultrarunning adventures such as the Born to Run 100, a one-hundred-mile trail running race; the Grand Canyon forty-seven-mile Rim-to-Rim-to-Rim run; and the ninety-six-mile trail run around Mount Rainier. Most important, he's a loving husband and father.

From Ron

Dustin is right. These principles have helped me reap rich results not only in my career but also in my personal life. But I wouldn't be who I am today without having him beside me, crushing his own incredible goals.

Here are a few things about Dustin you might appreciate knowing:

During Dustin's third year at Southwestern Advantage, he broke the company's all-time record, earning more than $100,000 during the fourteen weeks before his junior year of college. This feat landed him on *The Dave Ramsey Show* in an episode about college students who were graduating debt-free.

Dustin is the cofounder of Southwestern Consulting and president of Southwestern Coaching, which generated over $100 million in its first ten years and has helped more than fifteen thousand one-on-one coaching clients increase their income on average by over 25 percent.

Dustin has a psychology degree and has authored and coauthored multiple books, including *Navigate: Selling the Way People Like to Buy* and *Navigate 2.0*. He has been featured in *Entrepreneur* and *Fast Company* magazines, and in 2019, he was included in *Nashville Business Journal's* "40 Under 40" list of premier community leaders. At the age of thirty-six, he was named chief executive officer of Southwestern Family of Companies, the youngest CEO in the organization's 165-year history.

Dustin and I have learned a tremendous amount about human behavior, mindset, and results by personally coaching hundreds of top executives and leaders from numerous companies in nearly every industry. This work has been a blessing for us. Without a doubt, we know we were put on this earth to help people. But don't think for a moment that we haven't experienced failure, disappointment, and our share of discouragement along the way.

AN EPIPHANY ON THE WRESTLING MAT

A lot of people speak metaphorically about getting "beat up" by the world to describe a pivotal moment of decision. Those are the words I (Dustin) use too when talking about one of the first major turning points in my life. Except for me, there was nothing symbolic about it. I was quite literally taking a beating.

As a high school junior, I had made it to the Georgia state wrestling tournament as the last-ranked competitor in the 189-pound weight class. Just being on the state tournament roster was a major accomplishment, especially compared to the rest of my less-than-stellar childhood. I had always been the overweight, dyslexic kid who could barely pass from one grade to the next. Once I moved to Georgia with my family, though, I was finally able to take a step in the right direction. I lost thirty pounds, grew a foot taller, and got a chance to start over.

And yet, despite winning enough matches to qualify for the state tournament, I constantly wavered between confidence and despair. For every victory, I also endured a humiliating defeat. I couldn't escape the fear that my life would never amount to more than a mountain of losses. Before every match my mind was filled with a constant stream of what-ifs. What if I got hurt? What if I looked like a fool in front of a gym full of people? What if I embarrassed my coaches and my family?

In the past I had given myself permission to give up rather than give it my all and suffer a painful outcome. Giving up was the lesser of two evils in my mind.

Now that I had somehow reached the semifinal round of the tournament, I was convinced I would lose yet again. I was scheduled to face off against a wrestler who was everyone's pick to win it all—one of the best wrestlers in the state of Georgia. To make matters worse, he had already beaten me three times that season. Actually, that's an understatement. He hadn't just beaten me—he'd *destroyed* me in our last match together. He had literally lifted me off the ground and slammed me headfirst to the mat. When going up against this guy, my goal was not to win; it was to lose in the least humiliating way possible.

The match that day got off to a typical start. I saw no sign that the outcome would be any different. Several seconds in, I was on the verge of being pinned, but then something different happened. I snapped inside. I heard a voice in my head say, "If you give up now, you're going to keep giving up for the rest of your life." In my mind I saw scene after scene of me giving up, giving in, and losing. Suddenly all that pain, regret, anger, and humiliation reached a boiling point. I decided, "No! Not this time. There's nothing he can do that will make me quit!"

People in the audience told me later that I screamed "No!" and suddenly went after my opponent. I employed moves I had learned but was always too scared to try because I was afraid of getting hurt. For the first time ever, I gave 100 percent—and it worked! I lifted my opponent over my head and slammed him to the mat, and he had to take an injury timeout for the first time in his life. Minutes later I won the match, which advanced me to the state finals. Everyone was in shock—his coaches, my coaches, the crowd—but not me. A new sensation flooded my body. It was the rush of victory mixed with calm confidence, and I knew there would be no going back.

From that moment on, I had a confidence anchor (more on this later). I had faced my fears and conquered them.

I had redefined possible for myself.

A ROCK-BOTTOM MOMENT

Picture this: A forty-year-old man lies alone on the floor of a cramped apartment, sobbing. The place is not a home or a refuge. It's a makeshift penalty box where the man has been sent to pay for his failures and face his shame. Or so he believes.

It is the summer of 2013—and that man is me, Ron.

Until that season I thought I knew who I was: a purpose-minded businessman who could take pride in helping to build a stellar company spanning much of North America; a dedicated family man with a beautiful wife and four-year-old twin boys who were everything to me; and most of all, a man dedicated to God who believed he was put on this earth for a clear purpose. Not far away, near Seattle, my dream house was under construction, almost ready to contain the future that I had worked so long and hard to achieve. Professionally, I was someone who helped others succeed and reach their dreams. How was it possible that my own dreams were now in shreds around me on the floor?

I'd like to say my situation was something that made me unique or special, but I can't. Like millions of other people, I was experiencing an unexpected divorce that had turned my entire world upside down. I wasn't accustomed to failure, and my ridiculous ego was worried about what people would think of me—especially my kids. To top it off, money was tight: my production at work had dramatically fallen off since I had been focused on saving my marriage. Everything I had ever built, and everything upon which I had pinned my hopes, seemed utterly meaningless.

As I lay on that apartment floor in despair, though, I suddenly saw myself in a new light. I recognized that I had two new identities competing with each other. The first—the tear-stained victim—certainly had the upper hand at the moment. The victim inside me felt like the world was going to end (and secretly wanted it to).

But there was another identity struggling to take hold: the conqueror. I realized I could stop whining and wallowing and accept the potential for growth in the pain. The truth is, my divorce *had* happened, and I could choose how I let the experience define me. I could stop trying to figure out "who's fault" it was that our marriage had ended and start taking responsibility for my role in the situation.

That evening, I finally realized that *I* had the power to choose which path I would take. I could use my suffering as fuel to create lasting change.

That was the moment I redefined possible.

This powerful shift gave me perspective. I realized that while my circumstances were tough, they were not the end of the world. Eventually, the kids would be okay. Eventually, I would be okay. (In fact, we would all be so much better than okay!)

In the following weeks, I asked my ex-wife to forgive anything I had done to hurt her so we could pave the way for a good co-parenting relationship. I became more involved in church and surrounded myself with people of faith. I took up extreme trail running and set ambitious goals like completing the grueling Grand Canyon Rim-to-Rim-to-Rim run. I poured new energy and vision into my professional life, and soon I was on my way to breaking the Southwestern Coaching sales record.

Seven years later, I am happily remarried and have welcomed a beautiful daughter into my life. My boys are more precious to me than ever. I have earned a new, hard-won confidence in who I really am and what I'm capable of doing.

And all this happened because one night in 2013, I decided my pain would be fuel, not poison.

IF WE CAN REDEFINE POSSIBLE, SO CAN YOU

Helping people tap into their potential has become the highest calling of our lives.

We do it because we are a couple of regular guys who don't deserve anything but who have experienced the extraordinary power of redefining possible. We truly believe that if we can redefine what possible looks like in our lives, you can too!

The goal of this book is to give you the keys to a new future using proven strategies that will open possibilities that you've yet to imagine. We've already mentioned the RAFT technique that we used to redefine possible in our business and personal lives. In the following chapters, we're going to explore some foundational strategies that are based on seven key concepts: focus, ownership, vision, belief, confidence, faith, and impact. These ideas build on themselves in different ways to create a larger picture of what redefining possible means for you. Together, these strategies create the basis for a productive, balanced, and fulfilling life.

Starting from focus and ending with impact, the seven essential strategies detailed in this book can literally change your life:

- *Focus:* Focus creates power. Without focus, you will succumb to distractions, and your work will be much less effective. Being intentionally focused will help you get better results in less time.
- *Ownership:* When you take ownership of your life, you hold yourself to the highest possible standard. Taking responsibility for your actions will give you control and help lay the best possible foundation for future achievements.
- *Vision:* When you combine focus and ownership, you get vision. Vision is the fuel for your life. By casting a compelling vision, you will create energy, excitement, endurance, and empowerment.
- *Belief:* As others have said, your limits begin where your beliefs end. Your beliefs and convictions will help you break through barriers and self-imposed limits and find your calling.
- *Confidence:* When you create and harness unconditional confidence, you will know that you are enough. You will find peace in the face of adversity and learn to embrace your purpose.
- *Faith:* Belief and confidence results in faith. Faith helps you center yourself and identify your core beliefs to add conviction to your work and your life.
- *Impact:* We (Dustin and Ron) have strong faith in God, and we believe that He cares more about your impact than your accolades. If you want to redefine possible, your barometer cannot be the size of your house, how

impressive your job title is, or how many trophies are on your shelf. Instead, it should be how many lives you can positively impact.

YOUR FORMULA FOR LIFE

You are now standing at the starting line, moving away from complacency toward a new way of life. You're going to have to work hard, but with the ideas in this book, you will be able to power through. When you see obstacles looming, take heart. The rewards will come when you stay strong and committed to the plan.

Don't quit reading this book! Study these strategies and techniques; let them sink in. You might have to challenge a lot of the things you think are true, but getting "unstuck" is well worth the effort.

Stay on the path and avoid mental traps, like excuses, which will tempt you to put this book down and tell yourself you'll read it later. Be guided by determination and an eagerness to learn and grow. Stay open to change. When the lessons come, absorb them and take action. After all, we're talking about redefining possible for your life—and you only get one life to live, so now is the best time to start.

The key strategies we will explore in the pages ahead are elements in a formula that, when you grasp it, will change your life forever. Here's how the formula works:

Focus + Ownership = **Vision**

Belief + Confidence = **Faith**

Vision + Faith + Impact = Redefining Possible

There's a reason we've identified seven key strategies around these particular core concepts.

They work.

After all, without **vision**, you don't have direction. You just let things happen to you instead of being proactive. You're not on time, and you're not on top of the details. You don't follow through on your commitments. You lack focus. You are scattered, stressed, and overwhelmed.

When you don't have **faith**, you feel overwhelmed and hopeless. You're on edge, living in fear, always scared that something bad is coming just around the corner. Life without faith is full of shame, guilt, and worry.

It might be easy to see why you need vision and faith, but what about **impact**? Life without impact is lonely. You become so consumed by your image and self-serving goals, you don't see that people are hurting and in need. You are in your own world—and that's a lonely place to be.

If you see yourself in some—or all—of these descriptions, you may be concerned. But if you take only one thing from reading this book, please let it be this: *it doesn't have to be like that.*

If you are ready for them, the ideas in this book *can* transform your life. These are proven strategies and time-tested principles.

Think of this book as a practical guide on how to implement and live out these established ideas.

You've already taken the first step in your own quest to redefine possible. Simply by starting this book, you have put a check in the box by the first step to a new and better you.

The next step is to commit to finishing this entire book, no matter what. After all, two of the most insidious words in our vocabularies are *tomorrow* and *someday*.

This is your season, and now is your time.

It's time for *you* to redefine possible.

Sharpen Your Focus

*"Most people have no idea of the giant capacity we can
immediately command when we focus all of our resources
on mastering a single area of our lives."*
—Tony Robbins, best-selling author

I magine this: It's 5:30 in the morning when your alarm goes off. "It's Monday," you think. "Time to take on the week!" You've trained yourself to be an early riser, so you turn off the alarm right away, ready to take action on the plan you've created for the day. You pour yourself a cup of coffee and start the morning with fifteen minutes of meditation or prayer. After a healthy breakfast, you hit the gym and crush it.

Once at the office, you stick to a thoughtfully planned schedule that includes time for appointments, calls, brainstorming, and more. You are prepared for challenges, so when they come you tackle them with confidence. You're intentional. You're present. You're winning.

You feel joy. You feel alive.

Best of all, you have enormous, immense belief in what you are doing. You are productive all day, and people are drawn to you because of the positive attitude you exude. If you're recruiting, you find good people who want to be on your team. If you are selling something, you pitch your product or service with confidence because you know people want to do business with you. If you're giving a presentation, you do it with energy and positivity.

On the way home, you listen to a helpful podcast or audiobook. Then, before you walk in the door, you hit a mental "refresh" in order to be fully present and available. With your phone tucked away, you devote yourself to your partner or family. You sit down for dinner together. You listen intently as they tell you about their day, and you enjoy that quality time. Your schedule might even include having a sitter booked and reservations made for a date night with your partner.

Just before bed, you meditate or pray for a moment. You express your gratitude for all the little things that went right that day. You never take for granted the gift of life and the opportunity you have to help people every day through your work. When your head hits the pillow, you know you left it all on the field that day, so you sleep soundly.

Sure, you have some tough responsibilities, but you handle them with a light heart, a sense of joy, and enthusiasm. You're open to new goals, new dreams, new levels of achievement. Your relationships are rich and marked by genuine humility; your work life is satisfying and rewarded by prosperity and opportunity. You are known for your authenticity, never worrying about being someone you're not. You have mastery over your attitude, your activities, and your time. You let go of everything you cannot control. You are able to move beyond your mistakes.

On a deep level, you have a strong sense of purpose. You're increasingly dialed into the life you are meant to live. You feel fulfilled. You are driven by your own purpose rather than the agendas of those around you. Everything you desire in life now seems achievable because you have completely redefined what's possible.

Does this seem out of reach?

Many of the people we meet say that they are struggling to achieve the kind of purpose we've just described. They often have a good job, loving relationships, and a nice house. In fact, they may have all the material items they could want, but they're no longer *excited* about the things they've worked so hard to achieve. Their dream job has become simply a means of paying the mortgage—one more thing at the top of a long list of responsibilities.

If you're feeling tired, defeated by your circumstances, or unfulfilled in your work, you might have trouble believing that a different type of life is attainable. Fortunately, it's possible. There are strategies you can choose to employ that will unlock the kind of life we just described.

The first strategy we want you to embrace is to sharpen one of the most powerful tools in your possession. We want you to wield it every day.

It's your focus.

WHEN CRISIS HITS

I (Ron) learned how to maximize my focus during the most challenging trial of my life.

In the summer of 2016, my life was finally back on track. Three years had passed since that heart-wrenching night of despair, lying on the floor and feeling crushed by my divorce. I had found love again, and I was preparing to propose marriage to the new love of my life, Desireé. We were excited about blending our two families—her daughter, Hartley, and my twin sons, Van and Paxton (we call him P. K.). Professionally, I had regained my lost momentum and was building a thriving business. I felt stronger than ever before.

That all came to a crashing halt with one phone call.

In August that year, my son Van—seven years old at the time— developed what we thought at first might be an allergic reaction to shellfish. His face began to swell and kept getting bigger and bigger. When initial treatments proved ineffective, Van's mom took him to Seattle Children's Hospital for a more comprehensive evaluation. After a round of tests, doctors gave us horrifying news—three words that turned our world upside down.

"Van has leukemia."

I assure you that it is possible for time to stand still and for the earth to stop spinning. Suddenly, nothing else mattered as much as rallying to comfort and protect this little boy whom we all loved so much. We were thrown instantly into the overwhelming task of understanding this strange disease and coming to grips with what the diagnosis meant—for Van, certainly, but for the rest of us as well. What were his chances of survival? What treatments were recommended, and how would they affect him? How would our lives change as we rushed to provide Van with every possible advantage in the battle he now faced?

In November that year, Desireé and I got married in a small Thanksgiving ceremony. Van was there: thankfully, he was between treatments, so his immune system was strong enough to handle being around others. But the rest of the time was a blur of coping with hospital visits, making decisions about treatment options, and watching our boy suffer. On top of that, we had other children who needed our care and comfort, particularly Van's twin, Paxton, who had barely spent an hour apart from his brother in his whole life. In addition to the family stress, I needed to press on at work, which stretched my ability to focus beyond what I thought was possible.

It soon became clear to me what I had to do to survive this crisis. In the following months and years, I would need to truly embody what it meant to redefine possible in the face of hardship. I decided to be the greatest example I could be of strength and focus for my kids.

Here's what extreme focus looked like for me: When I was at the hospital with Van, I would pretend the rest of the world didn't exist. He had my full attention. When Van was napping, I would compartmentalize my pain and call my coaches and clients to support them. At home with the rest of the family, I'd think of nothing but being the best possible husband and father. The same was true with my career. I fiercely guarded work time against draining worries and distractions. I also kept a serious focus on my own mental and physical health, remaining committed to my personal fitness and sanity, making each workout count more than ever because I had no time to waste.

No one is ever ready to have a crisis like this, but when such a crisis does appear, it often comes bearing gifts along with challenges. That has certainly been true of this passage in my life. It has made me far more focused and intentional about my relationships, my faith, and my work. I have a much clearer view of what really matters in life and how to set appropriate boundaries and priorities.

Today, my family is thriving—and so is Van. In November 2019, three and a half years after he was diagnosed, Van was declared cancer-free and got to ring the bell at Seattle Children's Hospital, where he had been treated.

My experience with managing the difficult early stage of Van's illness showed me a new, unexpected, and deeper meaning of the word *focus*.

THE POWER OF UNRELENTING FOCUS

When we decided to write a book about how to redefine possible, we purposefully started with the concept of focus. We define focus as the state of being intentional and proactive—giving 100 percent of everything we've got. It's a big challenge for most of us, and yet it is the only reason that anyone accomplishes anything of significance. Without focus, we will be, as the saying goes, a "jack of all trades, but a master of none."

We see examples everywhere of what it means to lack focus. People want to get rich quick and lose weight fast; they want to keep up with their neighbors. Then they get bored with what they are doing as soon as they get good at it and decide to try something new.

We've had some very successful clients, and we've found there is a critical quality that sets them apart from the other people we coach. What is it? Our most successful clients are the ones who have learned to focus on long-term goals and concentrate over extended periods of time, regardless of what is happening at home or in the global market. This enables them to accomplish big goals by taking their long-term vision and turning it into reality.

Having sustained focus isn't easy. The world lacks focus. We live in a world of distractions, social media, and a twenty-four-hour news cycle. During Southwestern Coaching workshops, we often ask our audience, "What's your greatest strength?" Sadly, we've never—not once!—had someone answer, "I am good at focusing."

Most people go their whole life without learning how to go "all in" and give something 100 percent of their focus. And that's crazy.

Without focus, we get scattered and everything becomes watered down—a lesser version of what it could have been because we've done several things passably well instead of one thing with excellence. We get scared, we hold back, and we are often left wondering what would have happened if we had gone all in.

With focus, however, we become more intentional, which means that we get more done in less time. And with that extra time and laser-sharp focus, we can be unstoppable. As we mentioned, focus is one of the things that helped us reorient ourselves as a company in the early months of 2020 after the outbreak and the global state of emergency. When we utilized this strategy—along with the other steps in the RAFT technique—we were actually able to *increase* our activity levels from the previous year.

If you said, "I'm going to become a master at focusing," it would change your entire life. Because when you focus, you create power for yourself. It's like taking a magnifying glass and harnessing the power of the sun to create fire.

Humans are incredibly capable. Recent studies have shown that the human brain—which has around one hundred billion neurons and a quadrillion synapses that wire the neurons together—is even more powerful than scientists once thought.[1] But with all the technology and activities and choices that are available to us, we often become distracted, and most of us don't live up to our potential. If we could tap into the power of our mind and learn to *truly* focus, there's no limit to what we could do. We could change the world.

A SERIOUS CAR CRASH

It might seem strange that a man who was diagnosed with attention deficit hyperactivity disorder (ADHD) in college would write a book that includes advice on how to focus—especially since I (Dustin) am not talking about *focus* in any ordinary sense of the word. I'm describing the kind of hyper-focus that acquires the intensity of a laser beam, allowing you to achieve far more than you ever thought possible.

When I was first diagnosed with ADHD as a student at the University of Tennessee, I was briefly prescribed a powerful stimulant called Adderall, which is used to combat the effects of ADHD and chemically deliver the kind of focus we are talking about. For a while, it did just that. On the drug I found it easier to pay attention in class. I no longer needed as much sleep and could study all night if necessary. I felt superhuman! I might have continued to take it (and experienced the negative side effects that can come with daily use)[2] had it not been for an event that put me on a different path: a serious car crash.

One night a buddy and I were traveling back to Knoxville after visiting friends in Savannah, Georgia. He drove while I slept in the passenger seat. While stopped in a traffic jam, we were rear-ended by a car going seventy miles per hour. We spun around several times, and I awoke to the image of glass flying through the air. Before we came to a stop, the other car struck us three times, all on my side of the car. Fortunately, my friend and I were both wearing seat belts.

I could feel that my thumb was broken from hitting the console, yet when the police and paramedics arrived, I insisted I was okay and refused to go to the hospital. There was so much adrenaline—and Adderall—in my bloodstream that I honestly felt fine. As a young college kid, I had a false sense of security. The windows in the car were shattered and other parts were bashed in, but my friend and I still decided to drive home. We got in the car and miraculously made it back to Knoxville.

I did wind up in the hospital that night after my buddy called his mother to tell her about the crash, though. She immediately insisted we get checked out, having heard of someone who had died from internal bleeding hours after the adrenaline rush of a similar crash had worn off. The moment she said the words, I could feel the bruises where the seat belt had dug into my torso.

We found a hospital just in time. Whether from the Adderall in my system, the booze left over from the night before, or a mixture of both, I experienced severe—and terrifying—convulsions in the emergency room. Fortunately, the doctors were able to get my convulsions under control, and I was discharged from the hospital.

Yet despite the physical reactions I experienced from the Adderall, I continued taking the stimulant. For months I would lie down to sleep at night and instantly feel all the symptoms of a heart attack—tightened chest, shortness of breath, and rising panic. During the day my temper became short, and I started picking fights for no reason. I hardly recognized myself and had no clue what was happening to me.

Then a random thought crossed my mind: I wondered if I could I be suffering from a dangerous combination of Adderall and post-traumatic stress from the accident. I can't explain why, but I felt strongly that I had found the answer. (I subsequently learned of a Pentagon study that linked drugs like Adderall to more vivid recall of traumatic events.[3])

I stopped taking the drug, knowing it meant going back to square one in the search for a way to control my ADHD. In the coming weeks and months, however, I discovered some of the techniques we are about to share in this chapter—and they worked! That year I earned the best GPA I'd ever had in college and broke the sales record at Southwestern Advantage.

Take it from me: focus is possible, no matter what your situation.

FOUR TECHNIQUES TO SHARPEN YOUR FOCUS

When we coach leaders and executives, we walk them through four actions they can take that will strengthen their ability to focus as never before.

In fact, if you sharpen your focus starting today, within a week you'll see a noticeable difference in your productivity. Here's how to begin putting these four techniques into practice:

1. Eliminate mental clutter.

It's essential to recognize a primary enemy of focus: mental clutter. In fact, we cannot overstate the roadblocks that are created when we allow clutter to accumulate in our mind. This kind of clutter comes in many forms:

- *Too much incoming information.* This can be from the twenty-four-hour news cycle, social media, television, radio, emails, texts, and any number of other things.
- *An overcrowded calendar.* This results in filling your brain (and hours) with more obligations than you can possibly keep up with, which takes your attention away from your income-producing activities.
- *Unresolved conflicts and issues.* These challenges will weigh

on you and erode your peace of mind.

- *The daily drumbeat of distractions.* These can include work emergencies (or nonemergencies), demands from family, phone calls out of the blue, text alerts, and last-minute meetings.

The fact is, our culture and lifestyle seem intent on consuming every last kilowatt of our brainpower. All of these things can divert our focus from our highest priorities and our primary calling in life.[4]

Here's the good news, though: When you are intentional about cutting down the clutter, you will not only feel calmer, you will rebound from setbacks more quickly. You will have a sharp focus so you can think more creatively. You will also be more pleasant to be around.

To clear the clutter from your mind, we recommend writing down your to-do list, schedule, and other items you worry about forgetting. In general, you won't be able to hold conversations or even sleep as well when you have thoughts that are weighing on you. When you write these things down, you will see how much easier it is to concentrate. Odds are, you will resist this idea because it is a pain at first. Because it is not yet a habit, it will be uncomfortable. But this is a key step.

In addition to writing down your to-do list and schedule, we recommend keeping a journal for all your random thoughts and setting limits with your electronic devices. We're not saying you should completely cut out social media, the news, TV, or any other methods that you use to keep in touch with the world—but we do encourage you to limit the amount of information you consume and not to let what you see on those platforms clutter your mind.

2. Choose your targets.

Next, to bring more focus into your life, write down your goals and plans.

As professional sales and leadership coaches, we have asked thousands of high-performing executives to send us a copy of their goals. It is shocking to us how many people know conceptually that they should have their goals in writing and yet have not done so. We can't emphasize enough how important this is. We've found that very few of our clients who don't put their goals on paper have viable plans for how to achieve those unwritten goals.

Once you've written out your goals, you'll want to bring them into focus. The first step to doing that is to decide what you really want out of this one life you've been given.

What do you want in your personal life? What do you want in your business/professional life? What do you want in your spiritual life? After you've asked yourself these questions, stop reading this book and take fifteen minutes to write down what you want.

Then, the next question you should ask is, "Do I want it so badly that I am willing to focus on it?" When your answer is yes, then the magic happens. Now you can start to transfer your goals from a piece of paper to your calendar, giving yourself action items and deadlines.

For example, if your goal is to lose weight, you know that you need to eat better or work out more often. By putting your workout times in your schedule, you will be more consistent about actually showing up at the gym. And having a written workout plan will prevent you from wandering around the gym aimlessly—or worse, giving yourself an excuse not to make it there at all. Instead, you'll know the exercises you have to do when you're there, and because you are focused, you'll be able to get the same workout done in thirty minutes that used to take you an hour. Similarly, by having a specific meal plan to follow, you will meet all your nutritional needs and won't find yourself absentmindedly eating snacks. Grocery shopping for the week will also save you time and money.

What empowers you to make that kind of shift?

Focus.

Picture an ideal week in your life, define the related tasks, and then pencil them into your calendar. This can be done on paper or with an Excel spreadsheet or calendar app. For now, be sure to include everything you need or want to do for work, for yourself, and with your family.

It's crucial to be specific. Taking shortcuts or being vague will drastically limit your results. When you start writing down your schedule, set hard start and stop times for time-consuming activities, such as checking email. You'll soon find that you get more done when you know there is an end in sight. Beware of mental traps, such as telling yourself, "Yeah, I'll do it over the next few hours while I finish other stuff." Being intentional about your schedule and blocking out time for specific tasks will make it much easier for you to focus on what is most important. You will also accomplish more throughout the day instead of leaving lots of tasks halfway done.

When you're planning your week, beware of a second trap that we can all fall into: the horrible disease called "terminal uniqueness." When you are suffering from terminal uniqueness, you allow yourself to believe you are so different that your situation allows you to be an exception. You give yourself an out. The reality is that you are usually not that different. Everyone has a reason to skip or avoid applying these tried-and-true principles. Force yourself to follow through and make it happen.

Once you start scheduling the action items that will help you reach your goals, you'll find that every minute matters more and the minutes you invest will bear more fruit.

3. Guard your momentum.

After you have transferred your plans on paper to specific action items in your calendar, the next step is to stay accountable. Find ways to stay committed to the plan so you can continue to gain momentum.

You can start by protecting your schedule. This is especially important when you're working from home. Keep each task or appointment sacred, as if you were a Rottweiler guarding a bone. Do everything you can to prevent that task or commitment from being infringed upon by unplanned interruptions. If you find that your excuse for why you cannot get things done is because other people are "interrupting your day," then *you* need to be the one to make changes. Psychologists and best-selling authors Drs. Henry

Cloud and John Townsend explain that we are always conditioning other people and setting boundaries for how they act and communicate with us.[5] When something is important to you, you will create limits in your schedule, getting whatever needs to be done in the time you allot for it. So if your goal is to leave the office or shut down your computer at home by 5:30 every day so that you can eat dinner with your family, then you need to guard that time. Start work early. Make sure your meetings are efficient. Minimize interruptions. And then at 5:00, begin planning what you need to do the next day so you can finish on time.

Continue to exercise your follow-through muscles, which are just like other muscles: they grow when pushed. Your ability to carry out tasks and stay consistent will improve as much as you let yourself believe it will. As you stay motivated and keep yourself accountable, you will surprise yourself and get better at staying on task.

4. Speak your new reality.

Use affirmations to harness your self-talk. When you say empowering statements out loud, you will rewire your brain to believe that focus can and will be one of your greatest strengths.

Study the stories of many great and elite performers—whether they are world-renowned surgeons, historic artists, company founders, or Olympic athletes—and you will likely discover that they practice positive affirmations that lead to thoughts that create excellent results. Our thoughts direct our life,[6] so it's essential to have a list of healthy affirmations you can recite. These statements will adjust your thoughts so that they serve you rather than hold you back.

If you have struggled with using affirmations in the past, don't worry. We will provide ideas to make them work for you. We believe affirmations are so important, in fact, that we have concluded each chapter with targeted lists of what we're calling "power statements" to give you a head start. (There are also lines for you to write out your own affirmations.) You can learn to make affirmations feel authentic and meaningful. Of course, it takes sustained effort. Practice saying these statements out loud. Modify the phrases until they feel natural to you. Once you've mastered a few affirmations, add some new ones.

Learning to say affirmations to yourself consistently is a foundational habit. If it is awkward or you struggle at first, don't give up. This is a pursuit worth working on forever.

POWER STATEMENTS

As you learn to focus, try practicing the following affirmations:

"Focus gives me power."

"I was created to focus on helping other people."

"I am calm and focused in all that I do."

"I choose to focus on the things I can control."

"I'm locked in. Nothing can derail me from reaching my goal."

"My time is precious; I make the most of every opportunity."

"I'm present with every person I talk to."

"I spend my time and energy on meaningful things."

"I let go of any unnecessary worries or habits that distract me from my goals."

_____

_____

_____

_____

_____

_____

_____

_____

_____

_____

_____

SPOTLIGHT ON STRATEGY #1:

Tyler Hjelseth Sharpens His Focus

Imagine that becoming your best self and meeting your specific goals is like taking a cross-country road trip. You map out a route, tune up the engine, and fill up the tank. Then you put the car in gear and hit the gas.

As soon as you leave the driveway, though, a big juicy bug splatters across the windshield, followed by another and another. Before long, your focus has shifted from the road to the smeared mess in front of you. Even if you manage to reach your destination, chances are you'll be stressed and exhausted.

Now you have a picture of what happens when you let daily distractions (bugs) divert you from your plans. Fortunately, it's never too late to pull over, clean up, and get back on the road, this time avoiding the bugs entirely.

Tyler Hjelseth's story is a great example of just how beneficial it can be to refine your focus.

When I (Ron) began coaching Tyler in 2015, he was a moderately successful financial advisor with Northwestern Mutual Wealth Management Company. His production numbers were better than average, but nothing that would get him noticed beyond his home market of Tacoma, Washington. He wanted much more than that but was short on ideas as to how to get there.

One of the first things I advised him to do was keep a time awareness log. The goal was not to become a slave to the clock. Rather, it was to use the log to make every minute count. Tracking every block of time during his day was a hassle, but Tyler had a strong vision and purpose, and he was dedicated to doing it.

It didn't take long to realize one of Tyler's biggest disadvantages was self-imposed: he often let distractions and a relaxed approach to his schedule rob him of precious minutes. By keeping a log, he was able to see what it cost to schedule time for making prospecting calls and then let it slip away by answering a non-urgent email, updating his fantasy football lineup, or stopping by a colleague's office "just for a second." Those choices not only cost him time but also stalled his momentum, resulting in lost opportunity.

Tyler quickly learned to see the value in a single minute and to guard each one. "I saw that if I blew ten minutes, I might as well tear up a $20 bill," he admitted.

Next, I helped Tyler see that he also lacked focus in how he selected his clients. By trying to attract anyone and everyone as a client, he would never reach his goals. Setting his sights on a higher-caliber client— and giving his new team members the clients who had a lower net worth—meant changing his mindset and narrowing his focus.

To help him do that, I said, "Brother, if I came into your office right now and handed you $250, what could you do with that? Are you likely to throw it away?" No one would want to toss $250. And yet that's what Tyler was doing every time he spent two hours in a client meeting that had very little potential rather than building up his team to handle the client load and then delegating those opportunities so he could focus on his target market of business owners, executives, and physicians.

As our coaching relationship developed, Tyler became much more careful in screening and solidifying his own potential leads. By the end of his first year of coaching, he had nearly doubled his production totals and led all Northwestern Mutual advisors for new clients in his region. In 2016 his production nearly doubled again, and he was once more named a New Client Leader. Then in May 2018—still not yet thirty years old—Tyler qualified for Northwestern Mutual's Forum Symposium, an elite group of the company's top 2 percent of advisors.

I often saw myself in Tyler while coaching him—not in a flashback to when I was also in my midtwenties and in need of more focus, but to a more recent time. It was a reminder that achieving optimum focus is a daily practice none of us ever outgrow.

[STRATEGY TWO]

Own Your Past, Present, and Future

*"Responsibility equals accountability equals ownership.
And a sense of ownership is the most powerful
weapon a team or organization can have."*
—Pat Summitt, legendary basketball coach

Anyone who has been in a leadership role knows to be wary of the things "you don't know that you don't know." It's called having a blind spot—and all sorts of unexpected truths can hide there.

Like all people, leaders are prone to habits that can hamper team effectiveness, but they can easily remain unaware of those bad behaviors unless they ask hard questions and open themselves up to tough answers. It's intimidating to ask for feedback. But without that openness, team members rarely have the chance, or feel safe enough, to offer feedback about the boss.

At Southwestern Coaching, we encourage our coaching clients

to assess their leaders using a simple survey called the True-You Interview (included in the back of the book). In late 2017, I (Dustin) decided it was my turn to practice what I preached. I took a deep breath, pushed my ego aside, and sent a survey to all of Southwestern Consulting—including my team members, family, and friends—asking for anonymous feedback about myself.

Here are the exact questions I asked:

- What are my strengths? What do you see as my strengths in everyday life and business?
- What are my weaknesses? What doesn't work about the person I am being?
- How can I improve as a leader? What do other people count on me for? What do other people know I can't be counted on for?

Like most leaders, I knew it would be tempting to only take ownership of the positive things about myself and my management practices. That's easy. But true ownership means honestly facing those things that need improvement or that need to disappear entirely. The pursuit of excellence always involves clearing roadblocks, even ones that are highly personal.

Asking for that feedback wasn't easy. I'm not going to lie—before I started reading the results, I drank a beer. Then I cut a big slice of humble pie and took a bite with every completed survey I read.

Out of 130 surveys sent out, forty people responded.

At each end of the spectrum were responses that I knew I

could safely ignore. This is true for all surveys. Some people will decide they don't like you, no matter what, and take the opportunity to unload a long list of grievances. Others will think you hung the moon and share nothing but glowing praise. But in the vast middle there may be feedback that shows up again and again. Those are the clues you are looking for.

For instance, several respondents complained that I was consistently late for calls or meetings. After reading that feedback, I thought, "They're right! That's unacceptable, and I need to focus on this until it's fixed." I already knew that someone who routinely keeps people waiting is in effect saying, "I'm more important than you." And yet I had developed a blind spot and couldn't see that behavior in myself.

I took the feedback to heart by starting to build in a ten-minute buffer between all my calls and meetings. I enlisted my assistant's help so she could keep me accountable.

Fighting ego and accepting constructive criticism is one of the biggest challenges to taking ownership. But if I can do it, anyone can!

THE IMPORTANCE OF BEING ACCOUNTABLE

Taking ownership means accepting personal responsibility for your actions—whether the results are negative or positive. It means admitting when you mess up and embracing ownership of the way you spend your day, the choices you make, and the plans you have for your future. It means letting people know that you are going to follow through, execute your plans, and be accountable to yourself and to others.

Taking ownership isn't always easy. But *not* taking ownership comes with its own kind of pain.

When you don't take ownership of your mistakes, you can't take ownership of the good things in life either, such as your positive choices and the plans you've made for your future. And if you don't own your past and your present, how can you have a clear vision of the future?

Not only that, avoiding responsibility for your failures takes a lot of effort. You can easily spend more energy escaping responsibility than embracing important things like your mission, vision, values, and principles. When that happens, you set yourself up to feel like a failure. Shame and guilt can creep in as well as self-pity and self-absorption.

Taking ownership means that you are willing to listen and not get defensive when your partner tells you he or she feels ignored every time you pick up your phone during a meal. It means that you are willing to examine the truth behind the negative feedback you received at work rather than point out what your coworker is also doing wrong. It means that you are willing to grapple with uncomfortable truths about yourself—that maybe you have been self-centered, or too focused on work, or abrupt with your close friend or roommate. It also means you are willing to make changes and ask the people you have hurt for forgiveness.

Taking ownership may sound like a lot of work, but it is freeing. This is because, as you become accountable for your own past and present, you naturally stop making excuses and blaming others, and you start owning up to your mistakes and fixing them when possible. In fact, when you take ownership, you naturally find yourself doing what you say you are going to do, staying accountable, and making choices out of integrity rather than avoidance. You begin to feel as though you are living up to your calling and your potential, perhaps for the first time ever. And you earn the respect of the people around you, which is rewarding on so many levels.

How do you own your past, present, and future? The powerful strategy we want you to embrace is simple: say no to familiar lies and yes to empowering truths.

Let's start with the lies.

FIVE FAMILIAR LIES THAT KEEP YOU STUCK

When people avoid taking ownership, they rationalize their actions. *Merriam-Webster* defines rationalization as "a way of describing, interpreting, or explaining something (such as bad behavior) that makes it seem proper, more attractive, etc."[7]

We like the idea of breaking down the word *rationalize* into "rational" and "lies," because that's what you're doing when you rationalize: you're being dishonest with yourself or with others.

Think about some of the rationalizations you may have heard—or embraced—recently:

1. "Everybody does it."

This is one we've all heard since we were little kids. I (Ron) hear it all the time with my kids: "My *brother* (or sister) did it!" When we say this, we think it justifies what we're doing: If you're always showing up fifteen minutes late to work, then I can come in late too. If you're not totally honest about how much work you did on a group project, then I can fudge my efforts a little bit too. If you're taking more than your fair share, then I will too.

If my coworkers, friends, and neighbors are doing it, then it must be okay!

But having integrity and taking ownership of your actions is not about being comfortable with the way things are or what everyone else is doing. It's about embracing the way things *should* be. Taking ownership means that your ethics are all that matter. No one else's standards should be important. If you're constantly comparing yourself to what everyone else does, you're going to fail to take ownership of your life.

Redefining possible is about recognizing that "everybody else does it"—and then choosing to go in the opposite direction.

2. "It's not my job."

This rationalization combines avoiding responsibility with passing blame. It might show up when you start finger-pointing at a client, a friend or family member, or one of your team members.

As we said earlier, taking ownership means taking responsibility. It also means going the extra mile without looking for credit—and making this a habit. Sometimes you may have to do things that are below your pay grade. But the goal here is to exceed the expectations of your coworkers, your boss, your kids, and your partner. You should care so much about them and their expectations that job descriptions and compliments don't matter to you.

You may not be rewarded or noticed in the moment for taking on additional or unwelcome tasks, but the benefits will always come back to you. As Cindy Johnstone, the executive vice president and treasurer of Southwestern Family of Companies, often says: "The people doing the work always get the reward. Sometimes now, often later, but always eventually."

3. "I'm only human."

Average people are willing to take themselves off the hook so quickly. It's easy to do that—we *are* only human. None of us are perfect. (Of course, neither were the people we often hold up as heroes, such as Dr. Martin Luther King Jr., Mother Teresa, and Nelson Mandela.)

But this book is about not being average or settling for mediocrity. If you want heightened results, you have to think in a heightened way. Just because someone isn't a superhero doesn't mean he or she gets to bend the rules or give up. When you take ownership, you become accountable for every choice you make— *because* you're human. You own your life and your decisions. You listen, plan, take responsibility, and do the right thing. You say, "I'm going to give my best every single day and not make excuses. I know I'm going to mess up because I'm not perfect, but when I do, I'll learn from my mistakes and try not to repeat them."

As humans, we tend to judge ourselves by our best intentions. But in the end, we'll be judged by our worst acts—the areas where we cut corners or the things we discounted because we told ourselves, "It's just human nature."

4. "It's not important."

People use this rationalization when they want to qualify their actions or blow them off. But little things eventually become big things, and if you don't own the little things, you'll be even less likely to own them when they grow to become major problems.

Take lying, for example. Dishonesty can start small, like telling your boss that you were in off-site meetings and appointments for the whole afternoon when you really came home early and took a nap. But if you believe that a few missed hours at work aren't important, you'll be more likely to tell yourself that cheating on your taxes or even your partner isn't that bad either.

We believe that, as the Bible says, if you are responsible and diligent with the so-called little things, you'll be given more (see Luke 16:10). And if you want responsibility, if you want to live a significant life, if you want to live out whatever your definition of success is, you will understand it's the little things that matter most.

Or, to take it one step further, once you start taking ownership, you'll see that nothing is really that small. It's *all* important.

5. "But I am/have _____." (Apply label here.)

"But I'm tired," "I don't have enough energy," or "I have ADHD/dyslexia/a bad memory/fill in the blank here." People love labels. They may hear something a parent, friend, or doctor said about them, and suddenly they have adopted a label they can use for the rest of their lives to rationalize why they can't do something.

When people make these excuses, it's because they don't have a strong enough vision, they don't have clarity about their goals, and they lack the dedication to follow through on their commitments. Obviously, we all experience periods of time where we feel anxious or tired or scattered or forgetful. But many of us like to paint a picture of why we're special and unique and different—and then use it to justify why we can't do something. It's important to take ownership of any shortcomings you may have used as an excuse. Owning that you have ADHD, owning that your energy levels are down because of overwork, owning that you can't remember small details is a big step toward redefining possible. Once you take ownership of these labels, you'll find that you're able to move past them, overcoming any hindrances they might usually put in your way.

In his book *David and Goliath*, Malcolm Gladwell points out that 30 percent of entrepreneurs have some kind of ADHD or dyslexia. But those entrepreneurs overcame their perceived weakness to create highly successful businesses. Interestingly, Gladwell also points out that an equal percentage of people in prison have ADHD or dyslexia.[8]

It all goes to show that you create your reality.

USING AFFIRMATIONS WILL SET YOU FREE

I (Dustin) learned about taking ownership of my limitations—and transforming my attitude—when I was in college. During my first year with Southwestern Advantage, I was embarrassed when

I had to read out loud in a group. "I'm not naturally that good at reading out loud," I said, "so just have the next guy go." Later, my sales manager pulled me aside and told me, "As long as you say that out loud and affirm that you're not good at reading and writing, you'll never be good at it."

That was the first time I realized I'd been telling myself for my whole life that I wasn't good at something. It wasn't until I adjusted my self-talk—and literally changed the way I thought and spoke about myself when it comes to reading and writing—that my life transformed.

After the conversation with my sales manager, I created a list of affirmations. I wrote things like, "I am a wordsmith," "I have a vast lexicon," "I love reading," "I love writing," "I'm the best Scrabble player in the world," and "I am an author!"

Next, I started a Word doc and wrote anything that was on my mind. I also decided to start reading for pleasure. I read all the books I could find about sales and psychology. Then I discovered audiobooks and realized I could listen to books and retain all of the information.

Fast-forward to today, and this dyslexic guy with ADHD has now written three books—including the one in your hands—in part by harnessing the power of affirmations.

THE EMPOWERING TRUTH ABOUT YOUR WORDS

Affirmations are a tool you can use to take ownership of your life.

Affirmations need to be in the first person, using "I" not "we." They need to be in the present tense, meaning, "I am" or "I have."

These phrases should reflect what you are currently doing, not what you are going to do. And they need to include powerful words that convey emotions and create a picture in your mind. For instance, instead of saying, "I'm going to do my best," you might try stating, "I'm an unstoppable force!" These affirmations, or "power statements," will help you take ownership of your life every step of the way.

Affirmations work because, ultimately, words matter. There is a lot of science behind the use of affirmations. For example, a detailed study published in *Social Cognitive and Affective Neuroscience* concludes that affirmations can alter our neural activity and change our behavior.[9] An article in *Psychology Today* also indicates that people who practice affirmations are better at problem-solving.[10]

Practicing affirmations is one way you can do some self-coaching. Affirmations are one of the most effective ways to break through negative thought patterns and rewire your mind. Your thoughts and your words alter your behavior and actions, which affect your results—which then, in turn, transform your reality.

Affirmations can be a valuable anchor for you. They are constant, and they are what make every principle in this book sustainable. As the late motivational speaker Zig Ziglar was known for saying, "People often say that motivation doesn't last. Well, neither does bathing—that's why we recommend it daily."

Be prepared that your mind might actually fight you in the beginning. Changing your thought patterns will be difficult at first, but your brain is surprisingly adaptable.[11] So make a commitment to redefine possible by pushing outside your limits and breaking through complacency.

You can let the people surrounding you, as well as the news, society, and the world itself, program you to think a certain way. But if you let the outside world dictate your thinking, you'll never take ownership of your own life. The best path? Take control of your thoughts with affirmations.

Once you have your focus honed and your sense of ownership in place, you have a great opportunity to develop a clear and effective vision.

POWER STATEMENTS

When you rewire your brain to speak the truth rather than lies, you are essentially recreating what's possible in your life. Here are some affirmations we've found helpful for taking ownership:

"If it's meant to be, it's up to me." (See Robert Schuller's similarly titled book on positive thinking.)

"When I say I'm going to do something, I do it, no matter what."

"My word is my bond."

"I own this day."

"I follow through."

"I can. I will. I'm going to _____."

"Every hour gets my best; every person gets my best."

"I own every part of my life, and I am better because of it."

"I know my strengths and weaknesses, and I use this information to make myself a better person."

_____

_____

_____

_____

_____

_____

_____

_____

_____

SPOTLIGHT ON STRATEGY #2:

Terri Rickard Takes Ownership of Her Career

Terri Rickard knows, more than almost anyone, the importance of taking ownership. Her father, an addict, was in and out of prison during most of her child-hood—and because she was named after her father and shared his fiery spirit, she often heard that she was "just like him." Terri was determined not to let others' expec-tations and her family's past dictate her future, though. As a young girl, with the help of her mentors, she took ownership of her life and excelled in school, becoming the first person in her family to graduate from college.

Terri continued that commitment to ownership in her career, creating a successful cross-departmental training program in her first job out of college. Despite her success, she felt led to pursue other opportunities. "So I started praying for direction and researching my options," she said.

Terri began looking for a job in business where she could learn and grow. After a few months, she got connected with Henry Bedford, then the chairman and CEO of Southwestern Family of Companies. When she met Henry and learned about Southwestern's mission to build people and help others, she knew she was in the right place. Henry hired her on the spot to be his executive assistant, and he became her business mentor.

Terri was initially hesitant about going into business; she had a history degree and knew little about being an entrepreneur. But what she lacked in business experience, she made up for in dedication and her commitment to taking ownership. Early on, Terri noticed that the family of companies lacked a cohesive travel strategy. Each company was using a different outside travel agency, and multiple employees were booking travel on their own. As a result, Terri recalled, "Southwestern was not tracking its full spend with specific travel suppliers, nor was it utilizing its volume to maximize supplier partnerships and discounts."

Coordinating travel and minimizing expenses weren't part of her daily duties, but Terri was eager to take ownership and find solutions. "For me, taking on other work wasn't a chore or a burden," she explained. "It was an opportunity to support and serve my colleagues, our business, and our mission." Working with the accounting department, she figured out how to streamline the travel process, going through boxes of paperwork and expense reports that were brought in from the warehouse. With Henry's blessing, Terri created an internal travel program for the company's (then) sixteen operating divisions, managing more than

$5 million in annual travel spend. Within just a few years of collecting company travel data, conducting intensive industry research, and perfecting the vendor contract negotiation process, she had achieved savings of over $500,000.

In 2016, Terri launched Southwestern Travel Group to help other businesses save money on group travel, focusing on conferences, incentive trips, and school trips. As president, she has worked to make Southwestern Travel Group a trusted travel solutions provider by offering custom travel experiences, complimentary client consultations, and detailed planning, all while maximizing value and convenience.

In early 2020, Southwestern Travel Group was on track to have its best year yet—and then COVID-19 upended the industry. "Suddenly," said Terri, "every booking was canceled or pushed to a future date." She soon realized she would have to take ownership of the situation and adapt. "I was quickly reminded of the RAFT technique, which I learned during my one-on-one coaching program with Southwestern Consulting," Terri remembered. "Once I was able to realize the event had happened and then accept my situation, I focused on the things I could control, like my attitude and my schedule. This helped me transform my situation."

First, she worked with her staff to settle all of the

company's open accounts. Then they began increasing communication, reaching out to potential clients to let them know Southwestern Travel Group would be there when they were ready to resume traveling. The staff also brainstormed new offerings for the company, such as virtual experiences that could be used to enhance the in-person travel experience. Despite the challenges, virtual travel is a concept Terri is excited to pursue. "At Southwestern, we are encouraged to never walk past a problem," she said. "We're continuing to find new ways to rebuild and improve our offerings. We take owner- ship by getting into the details of our business, and we find unique solutions that will serve our clients—both now and in the future."

Clarify Your Vision

"Create the highest, grandest vision possible for your life,
because you become what you believe."
—Oprah Winfrey, global media leader and philanthropist

N elson Mandela is an incredible example of someone who had vision—and who lived his whole life with that vision as his guiding light. In the mid- to late-twentieth century, South Africa was run by a very small minority group who ruled with an iron fist. Having gained South Africa's independence from Britain, the members of this minority group were like elite monarchs. They practiced apartheid, discriminating against nonwhites, creating unjust laws, and enforcing racial segregation. In response, the South African majority group began to organize strikes, demanding basic rights like being able to buy food and to vote.

Nelson Mandela, who was part of this oppressed majority group, had a vision to create a free South Africa. He launched a campaign of nonviolent protests and proposed nondiscriminatory legislation.

His vision was so strong that he was able to maintain it even through decades of imprisonment. From 1963 to 1990, Mandela oversaw the rebellion from his jail cell. He was able to control South Africa's economy and to organize strikes. He challenged racism head-on and forged the path for South Africa to find democracy.

Mandela's vision never wavered. People threw him in prison, tried to bribe him—and even attempted to kill him. But he never compromised. In 1993, he was awarded the Nobel Peace Prize for his work in ending apartheid, and in 1994, Nelson Mandela was inaugurated as the first democratically elected president of South Africa.[12]

THE VALUE OF VISION

We can all agree that Nelson Mandela had extraordinary vision.

But what does that mean? When we say the word *vision*, we're not talking about eyesight.

Vision is seeing a future that hasn't happened yet. Vision is the light at the end of the tunnel—the image that guides you even when things are dark. Your vision is the picture of what things will look like when you're living on purpose, hitting on all cylinders, and achieving your goals. When you create a powerful picture of the life you desire to lead, you begin to live out that picture as if the elements in it were already true.

With vision, you are able to do everything with more energy, more motivation, and more excitement. We think of it as a tool—the GPS that directs your path. A well-defined vision eventually becomes so true to you that it feels like a calling. Vision also gives you clarity and focus.

In contrast, life without vision is completely unintentional. Instead of taking action, you let things happen and then react. Your feelings run the show instead of your rational plans. Without vision, you can't see clearly, so you become distracted from your true goals.

Having a clear vision is crucial if you want to redefine possible.

Vision is particularly useful when making decisions or dealing with difficult situations, because people tend to have one of three reactions to adversity. The first group is paralyzed by it, the second group struggles through it, and the third group adapts to it and becomes stronger. What makes these three groups so different? Their response has everything to do with the strength of their vision.

The first group is made up of people who don't have vision. When they hit a wall, that is all they see. They get stuck, unable to move forward in any way. The second group of people have a goal but lack vision. A goal will only take them so far, though. When adversity hits, they will make an excuse for why they didn't succeed. The third group is comprised of people who have a clear vision. These people are unstoppable. When they run smack into the wall, they barely acknowledge it. Their vision is so crystallized that they immediately look for ways under, over, around, or through the obstacle.

The other day, I (Dustin) was on a conference call with someone who said that she had been having a rough year. "I'm so tired," she said. "I've been working so hard; I'm just exhausted."

When I heard that, I wondered what the woman really meant by saying she was tired. Did she need to take a nap so she would feel more rested? Or was she feeling mentally exhausted, discouraged, or burned out?

Burnout is common in the workplace, especially with our constant connection to our phones and computers. It can be a real issue if you allow it to be one, and we agree that it's important to recharge, take mental breaks, and listen to our body. Sometimes, however, it takes more than self-care to address burnout, and that's because it's not just the result of simply working long hours. In our experience, usually when our clients say something along the lines of "I'm so tired," they're not literally tired. What they really mean is they have a vision problem. That is, they don't have the vision needed to propel them through difficult client negotiations, unforeseen circumstances, long days, and other work-related challenges.

Lack of vision can be linked to other underlying issues. For example, if we experience something painful that derails us for an extraordinary length of time, then we might have a vision problem. If we give up quickly, struggle with motivation, are easily distracted, mentally check out, start work late, and cut out early, we might be lacking in vision.

Vision is not supposed to be easy, because we're working toward something big—something uncommon and extraordinary. Vision *should* be hard and scary. Our vision has to be more powerful than the strength of our excuses. As we saw with the story of Nelson Mandela, the strength of our vision is what allows us to overcome hardships.

A clear vision helps you determine what you want out of life and what steps you must take to reach your goals. With vision, you wake up early if you're a morning person, starting work before everybody else—or if you're a night owl, you work late, finishing after everyone else. With vision, you work smart, think creatively, problem solve, and come up with new ideas. Your vision is so strong that you think about it all the time. It's part of you!

When you create a vision that's crystal clear, it shines a light on your path. It guides you back every time you get off course and helps you see what's possible before anyone else does. It helps you redefine what's possible within your mind's eye so you can take action to make it happen in real life. Having an image of what you want to achieve allows you to move faster and become more efficient and effective. Once you get in touch with your vision, you become an unstoppable force. You think about your vision all the time. It becomes part of you!

In this chapter, we will teach you how to define your vision, write it out, and make sure it's easy to follow. Here are three tools to help you clarify your vision and begin to turn it into a reality.

TOOL #1: YOUR VISION WORKSHEET

Because the concept of having a vision is intangible, we want you to do something to make it concrete. Think of a trait or characteristic you would like to have. Maybe you want to be resilient or perseverant. Perhaps you want to be loving or servant-minded, to think big, or to overcome challenges. Well, that can be part of your vision.

To turn your vision into a more concrete plan, grab a pencil and paper and get ready to ask yourself some questions. You are going to make three lists, which have historically been called the "be-do-haves." Be-do-have is something that Stephen Covey, Tony Robbins, and previous great motivational speakers have talked about for decades. Here's the model:

Who do you want to be? First, make a list of ten characteristics that detail the person you want to *be*. Think of it this way: How would you want the people at your funeral to describe you? What characteristics or traits would you want them to mention? This is the essence of what and who you are as a person.

1. _____
2. _____
3. _____
4. _____
5. _____
6. _____
7. _____
8. _____
9. _____
10. _____

What do you want to do? Next, make a list of ten things you want to *do*. Think about where you want to go, what you want to achieve, or even what awards you want to win. Go crazy with these and think big. This should be *fun!*

1. _____
2. _____
3. _____
4. _____
5. _____
6. _____
7. _____
8. _____
9. _____
10. _____

What do you want to have? Finally, make a list of ten things you want to *have*. While your "be" and "do" lists are most important, this list will help you clarify your goals. It might include having a bigger house for your growing family, six months of savings for emergencies, or the latest exercise bike for when you can't get to the gym. Let your imagination flow and be specific and vivid.

1. _____
2. _____
3. _____
4. _____
5. _____
6. _____
7. _____
8. _____
9. _____
10. _____

It's important to make these lists in order of "be," "do," and "have." Many people want to jump in with the "haves," but the "haves" are the direct result of the qualities, habits, actions, and intellect you possess—the items on your "be" and "do" lists. You will first need to decide what type of person you want to *be* and then *do* the things that kind of person does so you can gain the things you want to *have*.

Your lists might look like this:

- I want to *be* fit, dedicated, positive, motivated, passionate, determined, disciplined, purpose-driven, intentional, resilient, and selfless. I want to be a loving partner, excellent parent, and reliable friend.

- I want to *do* that weight-training workout four times a week, wake up at 6:00 every morning, go to my place of worship every weekend, run a marathon, swim with dolphins, hike the Pacific Crest Trail, have date night every week, take two personal development courses, coach my son's baseball team, pay for an extended family vacation, and make senior partner at work.

- I want to *have* a larger house with an office where I can more easily work from home, an SUV with room for my son's baseball equipment, a balanced portfolio that can withstand market fluctuations, enough time to pursue my fitness goals, engaged family time, my name on three books, a cabin on the lake where I grew up, well-rounded kids, and a team at work to help me best manage my time.

The things you write on your lists then become tied to your actions. For instance, your lists will help you to see why getting out of bed earlier is going to help you reach your endgame. Here's how it works:

With your vision in mind, you wake up at a specific time, rising with purpose and with a plan—you don't just wander into the day. Because you already believe you're a fit person, you have a plan for exactly what to eat, and you enjoy a healthy breakfast. You do some sort of exercise, visualization, or devotional meditation. Your morning routine helps you get your head right before you go to conquer the world.

If you have a vision of being a selfless person, then during your day, you focus on service-oriented goals. You ask, "Who can I serve? How can I bring my product or service or idea to the world or to this person in a way that might impact his or her life?" You don't make the day all about your awards, your plaques, your problems, or your numbers.

The more you focus on your vision, the more you will *become* your vision. But you have to think about it before it can actually happen. Having a vision means having a plan: living with intentionality a year ahead, five years ahead, ten years ahead, and so on.

TOOL #2: YOUR VISION BOARD

Once you have made your lists, the next step in developing a clear vision for your life is to tie your words to images by creating a vision board.

First, think about examples of your "be-do-haves." Find

pictures that represent each item on your list. Then, once you have found those pictures, you can combine them in a way that is meaningful. Your vision board can include anything—such as quotes, words, or pictures—that gets you fired up about working toward your vision.

We want to warn you about a common mistake people can make at this stage. Sometimes people start by looking through magazines to find pictures that catch their eye and then using them for their vision board. The problem is that if you approach the activity this way, you are letting a magazine define your vision for you, and it will end up being a limited version of what you need or want. Instead, identify the kind of life you desire to lead and then find specific words or pictures to reinforce that vision.

For your vision board to be most effective, you need to make it as detailed as possible, thinking about the people, actions, and emotions that accompany a particular vision or goal. In fact, some psychologists prefer using the term "action boards" to focus on the actions needed to get that particular job, renovate your house, or complete your first marathon.[13]

Once your vision board is completed, use it! Having images of those goals gathered in one place will help you focus on what is important to you. Keep your vision board somewhere you can see it every day so that your vision is literally within sight.

For our own vision boards, we (Dustin and Ron) found pictures online, printed and cut them out, and glued them on poster board. It was simple, and our vision boards continue to be a powerful tool for each of us. We both have our vision boards prominently displayed in our offices so we can stare at them every day while we're working toward our goals.

But it's not just about hanging a vision board and calling it "done." To effectively reach the goals on your vision board, you need to associate those goals with specific actions.[14] So look at your vision board consistently each day, visualizing the steps it will take to reinforce your new habits. By doing this, you will activate the motor cortex of the brain.[15] Your vision board will become a trigger to motivate you into action.

That means you'll work harder, wake up earlier, stay up later, and do all the extra things necessary to achieve your vision. In fact, when your vision is strong enough, detailed enough, and meaningful enough—when it includes not just what you want to *have* but also who you want to *be* and what you are willing to *do*—you'll actually find that your subconscious mind starts working for you.

This exercise will help you perform activities that you might not like to do but serve your long-term vision. For example, if humility is part of your vision, you will be more likely to trade in your pride for the opportunity to serve others. Or if you aim to be a top salesperson, you'll be more willing to make prospecting calls even if you find them time-consuming and tedious.

As we've mentioned, most people think short-term and limit themselves by only performing activities they enjoy. People with vision, however, think long-term. They are willing to do activities they consider difficult or unappealing in order to achieve their long-term goals.

Ron's Vision Board

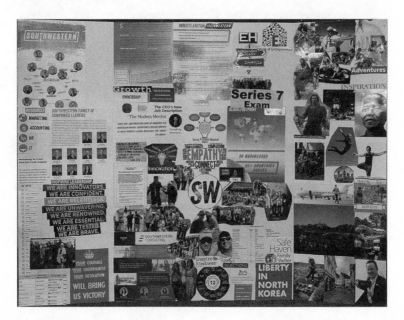

Dustin's Vision Board

TOOL #3: YOUR VISION STATEMENT

One way to crystallize your vision—after writing your "be-do-haves" and making a vision board—is to create a vision statement.

A personal vision statement will help you codify your vision for your life and articulate your destiny and why you were put on this planet.

Dustin's vision statement: "God gives me all strength, courage, and confidence. And with God anything is possible. He is the provider of all good things. My life mission and what God has called me to do is to help others reach their God-given potential every day."

Ron's vision statement: "I live my life to empower people, rise above adversity, overcome fear, and know what it truly means to serve others. Through a lifelong commitment to be the example, I will do my best to lead others, just as my Creator leads me."

To help craft your vision statement, look back on your "be-do-have" lists and the vision board you created. What is your vision statement?

My vision statement: _____

_____

_____

_____

_____

Remember that vision isn't just limited to individuals. You can create a vision statement with your family, your company, or people who share your spiritual beliefs, such as friends from your church or synagogue.

If you write a vision statement for your family, you and your partner may come up with your family's core values—the things you believe in as a family. For example, your family might be committed to respect, kindness, faith, trust, and community service. That's part of your family's vision. Then you can teach those values to your children as well.

You can also use this as a great exercise for your company's leadership team. Working within the company's core values, your team can come up with a vision statement that guides your work. At Southwestern Coaching, we encourage the entrepreneurial business leaders we coach to create a company creed or those in management to create departmental creeds for their team. This is a document encapsulating their company's vision, mission, values, and principles.

Our own Southwestern Consulting Company Creed lists a number of things that we believe in and what we strive to live by. You can read our creed on the following pages.

We've even created a Southwestern Consulting Leadership Pact that encourages our leaders to not only uphold the company's vision but also elevate their own vision and sales efforts so they can be an example and motivation to their teams. This role-specific vision statement encourages such responsibilities as recruiting, fiscal responsibility, professionalism, planning, and openness to feedback.

Here is our consulting creed:

THE SOUTHWESTERN CONSULTING CREED

At Southwestern Consulting we are based on 160-year-old principles. Our vision is to become the most trusted sales performance company worldwide. Our mission and the reason we exist is to help people achieve their goals in life. Our purpose for being in the sales performance business specifically is to help our clients elevate both the practice and perception of sales. As part of that pursuit, we believe in:

- Promoting the Southwestern story and its companies' philosophies to the professional world
- Being for what's right and not who's right
- Promoting principles more than personalities
- Being practitioners of everything we preach
- Providing workshops of real value and not just a sales pitch
- Seeing people not for who they are, but for who they can become
- Teaching sales people how to sell ethically, honestly, and without shortcuts
- Laughter and helping others to laugh
- Establishing a long-term relationship with each company and every person with whom we come in contact

- Making SWC a place of transformation from the inside out for our team members
- Providing unparalleled career opportunities for our team members
- Creating multiple revenue streams and intensive internal training systems for our team members
- Cutting-edge technological advancement and disseminating our information in a variety of mediums
- Challenging ourselves to continually learn, grow, and improve
- Giving the public quality information for free as a way of introducing ourselves and earning their trust
- Taking action and implementing suggestions that come from our customers and our team members

Most of all, we believe in being examples of success by operating with integrity, self-discipline, and passion in every area of our lives and our business. We are committed to building a company that creates a lasting legacy by building people. We are proud to represent Southwestern Family of Companies, and we will work continually toward helping people achieve their goals in life and becoming the most trusted sales performance company in the world!

Having a vision statement, written out and posted where you can see it every day, is a powerful tool that can help you achieve your goals. A vision statement is proof that you believe your life has purpose. It can give you the strength and endurance to fulfill your goals.

THE MYTH OF THE BALANCED LIFE

People sometimes ask us if it's possible to have focus, ownership, and vision and still live a balanced life. Recently, I (Dustin) was talking with one of my mentors, Dave Ramsey, after he was interviewed on Southwestern's *The Action Catalyst* podcast. Dave's take on balance is that it's a fantasy. It doesn't exist. No one doing anything great in this world is "balanced."

Ron and I agree. Everything happens in seasons. Understanding what period of life you're in helps you focus. Sometimes you have to intentionally "unbalance" certain areas of your life so you can pursue a vision that changes the world.

Elon Musk is a good modern-day example of someone who has an extreme vision that he lives out every day. He is a well-known billionaire entrepreneur who has a vision to accelerate the world's use of sustainable energy and return human spaceflight to the United States. Now compare Elon Musk with the late Mother Teresa, a Roman Catholic nun who gave up all her personal wealth and devoted her life to serving sick and poor people around the world. Mother Teresa was an incredibly different person with a *very* different vision. But like Elon Musk, she employed unwavering focus, taking ownership of her strong, powerful vision to make the world a better place.

As we reach the end of this chapter, we want to point out that vision completes one of the formulas in this book. Focus, which was the topic of chapter 1, and ownership, the topic of chapter 2, combine to create vision.

Focus + ownership = vision

How does this work? First, you master the ability to focus—to concentrate and eliminate distractions. Next, you own your situation, your abilities, your emotions, and your strengths. Then, you clarify your vision, bringing it into focus and making it your fuel.

Your vision is your calling. Your vision is something you will pursue your whole life. It's the reason you are on this earth—literally what you were created for and why you were born. You're here, reading this book for a purpose. Now it's time for you to carry out that vision.

POWER STATEMENTS

Here are some affirmations on vision:

"My endurance in life is directly tied to the clarity of
my vision."

"I know exactly what I want out of life and how to get it."

"Vision is the fuel that propels me forward."

"I inspire other people with my vision."

"I'm living out my calling; I'm right where I should be."

"I've got a vision for my life, and I won't let anything hold
me back."

"I'm prioritizing the activities that will help me achieve
my goals."

"I see myself having a successful business and authentic,
loving relationships."

"I claim the joyful future that I have envisioned."

_____

_____

_____

_____

_____

_____

_____

_____

_____

_____

SPOTLIGHT ON STRATEGY #3:

Virgie Sandford Clarifies Her Vision

Virgie Sandford, a top sales manager with Southwestern Advantage, was raised in Spearfish, South Dakota, by a family who taught her the importance of integrity, faith, hard work, and serving others. Yet she had never been exposed to the concept of *vision*.

She learned about it in college when she joined the Southwestern Advantage program. Selling was far out of her comfort zone. "I was a shy, small-town freshman who knew nothing about sales," she said. "In fact, I had worked my whole life to avoid rejection, so the idea of selling door-to-door was intimidating." But Virgie believed in the company's vision of building skills and character in young people, so she set aside her fears and spent several successful years selling educational products for Southwestern Advantage.

After college, Virgie stayed with the company because she wanted to provide other students the same opportunity she had been given at a pivotal stage in life. She and her sales manager decided she would move to Texas, where she didn't know anyone, to start a division of the company. The same week Virgie moved, however, her sales manager unexpectedly left Southwestern Advantage. "I had to remind myself why I had chosen this work in the first place," she said. "I still believed in our program's vision and knew I could grow here. When we are clear on our 'why' and our vision, it helps us weather life's disruptions and disappointments."

In 2005, Virgie had a much more serious disruption: a near-fatal car accident. She spent eleven days in a coma, suffering serious internal injuries and broken bones, and her foot was scheduled for amputation. Over the next few months, she worked daily to relearn to read, rebuild her memory, and be able to walk again. Skilled surgeons, prayer, a positive mindset, and a commitment to her vision helped piece her mind and body back together. Virgie felt like she was given a second chance at life, and she became committed to spiritual growth as an important part of her personal vision.

She returned to her position at Southwestern Advantage just six months later. The transition was more difficult than she anticipated, though. She struggled—her team shrank from 150 people in 2005 to 60 people in 2007—but with support from her loved ones, she reframed her vision, grew her sales organization, and became a top regional sales director. Over time, Virgie further developed her personal vision to be a "lighthouse" for others. "A lighthouse helps guide people to their goals," she explained. "I want to be a constant source of love, light, and truth for others."

In 2019, Virgie wanted objective guidance from someone who could help her fulfill her personal and professional goals. She hired Emmie Brown, one of Southwestern Consulting's executive-level coaches, because Virgie knew if she were *paying* for the advice, she would be much more likely to adopt it. Emmie challenged Virgie to more clearly identify her vision priorities—faith, family, health, and work—and build into her schedule specific activities related to each.

One of Virgie's family priorities was to maintain a close relationship with each of her fifteen nieces and nephews. She realized that this commitment required more than just an occasional trip to visit them in South Dakota, so she shifted her travel schedule to fly to South Dakota nearly every month and decided to start a 529 college savings plan for every child. She also finances "Travel with Aunt Virgie" trips with each child when they are in middle school, and then for high school and college graduations. This has been an opportunity to teach her nieces and nephews to build their own vision. "Even when they are in elementary school," said Virgie, "we talk about where they might want to travel for college graduation. They can pick anywhere in the world for that trip!"

Virgie's vision evolved over time. It started with latching onto a company's vision that she believed in, then creating one for her own organization, developing one for her life, and helping others create a vision for their lives as well. "Vision has to include things outside of work and possessions," said Virgie. "At the end of our life, that nice car won't be holding our hand. It will be the relationships that we have invested in that matter."

Strengthen Your Belief System

*"A person often becomes what he believes himself
to be. . . . If I have the belief that I can do it, I shall
surely acquire the capacity to do it, even
if I may not have it at the beginning."*
—Mahatma Gandhi, social activist and leader of
India's passive resistance movement

The first thirteen years of my (Dustin's) life were rough. I struggled in school, working harder than any of my classmates and still failing more often than not. The problem, I learned many years later, was that I was in the fight with one hand tied behind my back: as I mentioned earlier, I had undiagnosed dyslexia and ADHD. What seemed to come easily to others—like studying, reading, and staying focused—was a monumental undertaking for me. Without knowing the real cause of my struggles, I decided I was simply "stupid." Other kids concluded that as well and made fun of me every chance they got.

I was overweight and had no friends to speak of. I spent all my time playing video games and trying not to be noticed. My father owned a flooring business in Nashville, traveling and working long hours six days a week. His absence made it easy for me to believe he didn't value me any more than the rest of the world did. I didn't feel carefree like a kid should. Instead, I trudged through my days doing what I could to get by. Looking back, I've often felt deep compassion for that "soggy noodle" version of myself.

Then, at age thirteen, everything changed. I went to a church camp, and at an altar call at the end of one service, I went to the front of the sanctuary and gave my life to Jesus Christ. It was as if someone had reached into my heart and mind and flipped a switch. For the first time ever, I felt glad to be alive, and I was full of passion, enthusiasm, and joy. I got baptized, and a new sense of purpose flowed through me like electricity. I told everyone I met that they should go to church camp too!

Around the same time, my dad had his own "come to Jesus" moment at an event for Promise Keepers, a Christian parachurch organization for men. He saw the damage it had done to spend so much time on his business and so little on his home life. He came home and announced he was selling the company and wanted to start making amends and work on his relationships with my mom and me. That year we moved to Dalton, Georgia—and I grew a foot and lost thirty pounds. Suddenly, I had friends and was one of the popular kids. I went from soggy noodle to supercharged rocket practically overnight.

It took a number of years before my newfound faith in God was fully visible in my lifestyle choices, but my spiritual transformation was real and set the stage for every pivotal moment that was to come.

BELIEF IS YOUR FOUNDATION

Belief is the foundation on which our (Dustin's and Ron's) entire life is built.

Your belief system comprises the principles and values that are hardwired into who you are. You may have devout spiritual beliefs, such as an unwavering belief in God or belief in a higher power, or you might believe in love, family, or helping those in need.

When you have strong beliefs—whatever they are—you have strong convictions. When you have strong convictions, you have unwavering confidence. When you have unwavering confidence, you can do bold things. And when you act boldly, you get results. Having a strong sense of belief can help you break through limits and redefine what's possible for you.

As we often remind ourselves, "Limits begin where belief ends." And, to paraphrase Zig Ziglar, "It's not the height of my logic but the depth of my convictions that matters most."

Belief helps you to be innovative and challenge the status quo. When your beliefs fuel your actions, you have the energy to do more, and you can help the people around you see what they are truly capable of doing too.

Unfortunately, some people don't have beliefs that support growth. They may believe their life doesn't have purpose or that they are unimportant. Maybe something traumatic happened in their past or they just absorbed negative messages from society. Either way, these people feel limited. This isn't their reality, though; those limits exist only in their mind. And those limits can be changed by having a strong belief system.

Having the ability to believe in yourself starts at a young age. For example, children aren't born knowing how to swim. They usually start by learning how to blow bubbles in the water. Then they learn to dog paddle and swim different strokes. Over time, they are able to dive into the deep end, swim to the surface, and reach the edge of the pool. But children learn to swim not just because they have been instructed in the proper techniques—they do it because they *believe* it's possible to move through water and stay afloat.

Children pick up things more easily than adults because they haven't yet learned they can't do something. Unfortunately, as we age, society often conditions us to place limiting beliefs on who we are and what we can do. In high school, we hear that a four-year college is the only way to succeed in life. In college, we're encouraged to work a traditional, nine-to-five corporate job. As adults, we watch commercials that tell us that driving certain cars or trucks will show our neighbors that we've "made it."

If we're not careful, we'll make decisions based on what society tells us is normal. In our coaching work, we've found that many people just float through life, letting everybody else construct their belief system. They let social media or the news tell them how things should be, and most of the beliefs they *do* have are fickle instead of solid. For beliefs to really make a difference, though, they have to be stronger and better formed than that.

Ultimately, your belief system guides your decision-making, driving what you do or don't do. Having strong beliefs is at the heart of innovative work. Beliefs enable you to be in touch with your sense of the possibilities, know your own barriers, be honest about your goals, and stay positive even if you get derailed.

Shifting negative beliefs is a foundation for redefining possible.

BEWARE OF BARRIERS

Before you can use your beliefs to redefine possible, you must first make sure you are thinking with complete freedom. In order to do that, you need to be aware of belief barriers.

Belief barriers are assumptions that limit the action you would take to accomplish a goal. Limiting beliefs can play out in many ways, affecting how we budget, the way we accrue credit card debt, how—and whether—we ask for a raise, and how we approach relationships. Belief barriers might include thoughts that affect your work, such as, "I'll never make more money," "I don't have the right experience," or "No one's going to listen to what I have to say." They might include thoughts that impact your relationships, like, "I'm not good enough to date that person" or "I'm socially awkward; no one likes me."

It's amazing what happens once our belief barriers are knocked down. I (Ron) used to think a three-mile run was long, but once my beliefs changed about what I could do, I worked up to running one hundred miles!

If you line up ten people with the same amount of talent, you will see dramatically different results because of their varying belief barriers. Some of the people simply won't believe as big as others. But we'd bet every day of the week on the person who believes biggest. Although we don't know for certain who said it, we love this quote and cite it often: "If you think you can or you think you can't, you're right."

The good news is that your belief barriers can be broken—and you can start by stretching your beliefs. First, identify a personal belief barrier you want to demolish this month. Look at your vision board for your big goals and identify one thing that's not happening.

For instance, let's say your vision board includes a picture of a triathlon medal. Your goal is to compete in your first triathlon, but you've never done the swimming portion of the race. "I'm a great runner and cyclist," you tell yourself, "but I'm a weak swimmer. Maybe I should stick to marathons and bike rides instead." To break this belief barrier, you must shift from focusing on what you haven't done (competitive swimming) to reminding yourself that you are a strong, well-trained athlete.

Whichever belief barrier you choose to break, make sure it's one that stretches your abilities. Do something that intimidates you. Change your self-talk. Train hard to beat your own personal records. Then make it happen.

LIVING WITHOUT BELIEF BARRIERS

Once you get rid of belief barriers, the sky's the limit.

The best possible example of someone who breaks belief barriers is our colleague Henry Bedford, chairman of the board at Southwestern Family of Companies and the former CEO. Henry's belief in what's possible is off the charts.

Henry Bedford started his forty-five-year career with Southwestern as a college student, selling door-to-door with Southwestern Advantage. He was then hired by the company in 1976 as an internal auditor. At the time, Southwestern consisted of one company and one start-up called Nashville Educational Marketing Services, with total combined revenues of $25 million. Now, as of 2020, Southwestern Family of Companies consists of more than twenty-five companies across over a dozen countries and millions of customers worldwide—and Henry has been personally involved in acquiring and/or developing every single one of those new businesses. He learned from his mentors that if you run a company by the right beliefs and principles, you can figure anything out.

Henry's amazing belief and willpower extends to his personal life. He has been skydiving more than 500 times, including doing skydives out of hot air balloons. He owns a hot air balloon and has competed in and won international competitions.

From there, he got into riding motorcycles during his vacations. He started with one motorcycle, which he rode from the East Coast of the United States to Los Angeles, then from Los Angeles up through Canada and Alaska, continuing each year from wherever he left the bike the year before. He bought another motorcycle in Los Angeles and rode with a friend south through Mexico into Central America, across the Panama Canal, and down into South America, leaving his bike at the end of each journey, usually in the home or barn of a local he had befriended. He continued through Colombia, Ecuador, and Peru, riding his motorcycle over the Andes on goat trails or often with no road at all, and into the Amazon.

After that, Henry took up sailing. He bought a forty-two-foot sailboat, despite the fact that he had never sailed a large boat in his life, and taught himself how to sail by watching YouTube videos. He sailed through the open seas to Cuba, Grand Cayman, and then to Panama.

Henry also believes in helping others, a principle he says he learned from his mentor and former CEO Ralph Mosley. Over his career, Henry has found time to build Safe Haven Family Shelter in Nashville, Tennessee; has led the building of homes for needy families in the US, Mexico, and Guatemala; and has raised money to help North Korean refugees escape to freedom.

Henry is a great example that your belief can take you anywhere—when you have a clear vision. What are your goals and passions? If you don't have a clear answer to the question, it's okay. The answer will emerge. We like to compare this process to a scene in the movie *The Last Samurai*. In the film, Katsumoto (played by Ken Watanabe) asks, "You believe a man can change his own destiny?"

Tom Cruise's character, Nathan Algren, replies, "I think a man does what he can until his destiny is revealed."[16]

CHANGE IS PROGRESS

All of us believe in our gut that it's possible to do things we don't yet know how to do.

For example, if you play a sport, you didn't automatically know the rules of the game or the technique of how to play. You probably practiced, joined a team, or took lessons. But because you believed that you could play tennis or hockey or golf, you figured it out. Similarly, you weren't born knowing how to write research papers or solve complex math equations like you did in high school or college. Instead, you worked hard, studied, asked questions, and ultimately believed that you would eventually learn the skills required.

The point is, there are very few things that we just "know" how to do in life. Everything else comes through a lot of hard work, some natural skill, and having the confidence—the sheer belief—that we will be able to learn new things.

When you're starting to make a big change, setbacks *will* happen, whether you are learning how to manage your company's financials or just climbing on your bike for a workout. You might catch yourself thinking, "I'm no good at spreadsheets," "Man, I hate doing that exercise," or "I'm just no good at speaking in front of people."

Resist the impulse. Don't beat yourself up or indulge in negative beliefs. You'll just revert back to your old ways, and you definitely don't want to do that.

We have mentioned self-talk in other chapters of this book, but this is where it is truly crucial, because your beliefs literally reprogram your life. We have a saying at Southwestern: "Success comes from our actions; actions come from our feelings; feelings come from our attitudes; attitudes come from our beliefs; and beliefs are who we are."

At the beginning of this book, we talked about how we were able to steer Southwestern Consulting through the early months of the COVID-19 pandemic. The news at the time was doom and gloom, with stories about how the stock market was crashing and companies were being forced to furlough employees. It would have been easy for us to get caught up in that cycle of fear. But we believed completely in our work at Southwestern Consulting—in fact, we believed that our mission of impact was even more critical during the crisis than it ever had been, and that motivated us to take action.

If we had given in to the fear, you'd likely not have this book in your hands right now.

As you can see, your beliefs are the first ingredient in achieving success. Beliefs come from your programming and conditioning. What you think about all day is what you will believe. What you read and watch also influences your beliefs, so if you struggle with belief barriers, we recommend studying books like the Bible, reading inspiring biographies, watching motivational TED Talks, or listening to podcasts like *The Action Catalyst*.

You probably have beliefs that are not serving your best interests. When you can identify those negative beliefs that don't serve the kind of person you want to be, then you have taken the first step to reprogram those beliefs.

Your belief barriers will slowly start to dissolve when you examine your self-talk. Notice those victories and build on them. Catch yourself doing things right! Your success will compound if you build yourself up. Consider adding affirmations to support the progress you've made toward your goal and to help keep you accountable.

Finally, be aware of how you're feeling. You will inevitably hit a point where a challenge pops up and derails you. When that happens, you'll need something—like an affirmation or a helpful podcast—to keep you going. (You can also try using the RAFT technique in the back of the book.)

Don't be deterred. Look for progress, not perfection. Remember, this is not supposed to be easy. You need faith, perseverance to overcome, and affirmations that speak to your resilience. Forgive yourself, move on, and keep believing.

BELIEVE BIG AND CHANGE YOUR LIFE

When we burst through belief barriers, set big goals, and tackle them with gusto, we are building confidence that we can handle anything in life. And sometimes, when we are facing difficult things, we need that confidence more than ever.

I (Ron) was sitting with my son Van in the hospital one day during a chemo treatment when I felt tears start to roll down my cheeks. Between Van's battle against leukemia, my new marriage (Desireé and I hadn't even gone on our honeymoon yet!), our two other kids at home, and my responsibilities at work, I was overwhelmed. But I didn't want my son to see me break down. I wanted to be strong in front of him and show Van that, as a family, we could all rise above any obstacle that came our way.

I wanted to show him what it meant to take true ownership of my beliefs.

One of the things I did was set a big goal at work. My hand was shaky as I wrote it out. Even though I was behind in my sales goals because of being at the hospital so much, I vowed to break the company's all-time record for the most client sales in a year *and* become a senior partner by the end of 2017.

This turned out to be an even bigger challenge than I'd anticipated. I doubted myself nearly every day. I was constantly on the verge of giving up and had a lot of strong rationalizations for why I should let go of my goal. But I followed my plan. I tried not to make excuses. I kept to a strict schedule, staying focused and working my heart out when I was at the office, and then shutting off my phone and filling my heart again when I was with my family.

I spoke affirmations, telling myself, "Just stick to the plan. If this goal is in my heart, it must be true; it must be pure."

After my last workshop of the year in mid-December, I wasn't sure if I could reach my goal. I told Dustin, "I might have a shot to break the previous record, but I think one of our other coaches has done more."

I was starting to give up. "Maybe it wasn't meant to be," I thought. "Maybe I should just go home, be with my family, and get ready to celebrate the new year. I can always try again next year." But Dustin reminded me, "Finish strong. You never know what can happen."

I didn't want to break that record just to beat some number. I wanted to do it to change more lives! So, I looked at the wall in my office, where I had the faces of the people I coached posted prominently. I reminded myself that those people were fighting to improve their own lives. Even more exciting, I knew I was there to help them do it.

On December 29—the last business day of the year—I did it. I broke the record by signing up one more coaching client. That one day, that one extra call, that one client made the difference, enabling me to break the company record and finish number one in a team of top-producing salespeople. More important, I was able to be that example of belief for my three kids.

POWER STATEMENTS

These affirmations will help you see yourself as someone who has a solid belief system. You can use these affirmations to retrain your brain to burst through belief barriers and accomplish greater things than you ever imagined:

"I can. I will. End of story."

"I believe in myself and trust the process."

"I can do this."

"I've done it before, and I can do it again."

"I believe I can change the course of my life."

"I let go of all doubts."

"I cut through belief barriers like a warrior clearing a path in the jungle."

"I choose to believe in the good. I set aside negative thoughts that don't serve me."

_____

_____

_____

_____

_____

_____

_____

_____

SPOTLIGHT ON STRATEGY #4:

Will Bartholomew Expands His Beliefs

As a collegiate football player, Will Bartholomew seemed destined for a career in the National Football League. At the University of Tennessee, he played fullback behind legendary quarterback Peyton Manning. His team won the national championship in 1998, and he was captain as a senior. Along the way, Will captured a number of NCAA Southeastern Conference honors. In 2001, he signed a contract to play for the Denver Broncos as an undrafted free agent.

Then, in one moment on the practice field, he suffered a severe knee injury that sent him home to Nashville to recover. He would never again play professional sports—but a new path opened up for him.

During his recovery, Will realized, "There was nowhere for me to train like I did when I was playing for a Division I college team." So he decided to fill the need himself. He bought some equipment and opened a facility called D1 Sports Training. Other athletes were showing an interest in his program, and his success was growing . . . but he realized he needed help scaling the business to the size he envisioned. At the time, D1 was a small operation with four gyms, but Will knew it could be nationwide one day. That's when he contacted Southwestern Coaching, and I (Dustin) came on board to coach Will in putting sales processes in place to help grow the business.

Soon, Will's entire team was on board, too. After spending a month observing how D1 went about a number of critical functions—from sales to team recruitment to training—we identified several areas in need of improvement. First, while Will had spent a lot of time developing world-class training services and programs, he knew he needed help to get a sales process in place so he could get new clients and hit revenue goals. We created a number of selling and recruiting systems, processes, training manuals, and scripts to make the sales and recruiting operations more efficient and more effective, and we reverse-engineered their goals into the daily activities that would be necessary to meet them.

For example, we discovered that to recruit just one new athlete customer, a team member would have to spend three hours at a sporting goods store developing at least twenty leads, then follow up with phone calls to get just three people to come to the gym. From those three, one person would enroll. So we helped set up critical success factors—tracking systems that would recognize and reward sales and prospecting leaders.

The bigger issue, however, was trickier to address: the whole D1 team—including Will himself—was being held back by belief barriers. Early on, Will had decided to hire team members who were athletes because they understood sports training. The problem was, they didn't yet understand sales. For many, it shook their confidence and belief in their ability to succeed outside of athletics.

To combat this corrosive doubt, we went to work correcting their negative self-talk. As we explained to the D1 team members, what you tell yourself about your abilities determines your reality. More than just teaching hard skills like sales scripts and processes, we shared positive affirmations for each person to use to break their belief barriers so they could believe they would be just as successful at sales as they'd been at their sport.

We trained the D1 team on what true professional selling is all about, explaining that true salesmanship is about helping people, identifying a need, and helping fill the need. We helped them focus on asking questions, listening, and customizing their presentation to the needs of their prospect.

Once the team members had broken those belief barriers and better understood what it meant to be a sales professional, they were ready to embrace learning new skills, just like they had done as rookie athletes.

We created competitive incentives, weekly and monthly competitions, and daily and weekly technical trainings. Soon their belief in what was possible changed as they began to organically grow their sales revenues and became true sales professionals.

One small victory at a time, they revamped the company culture and learned to believe they could accomplish whatever they set out to do. When Will hired Southwestern Coaching, D1 was a small business with four locations. Today, D1 Sports is franchised, with more than forty open facilities and one hundred more in development around the country.

Cultivate Confidence

"You gain strength, courage, and confidence by every
experience in which you really stop to look fear in the face.
. . . You must do the thing you think you cannot do."
—Eleanor Roosevelt, First Lady, writer, and advocate

Few things will shake your confidence faster than teetering on the edge of heatstroke at the bottom of the Grand Canyon, nine miles and six thousand feet of elevation away from help. Especially when you know you have only yourself to blame.

But that's getting ahead of the story.

I (Ron) have been an athlete my whole life. As a kid I played every team sport available. When I got older, I could usually be found at the gym or city park, hustling in pickup games or on some recreational league team or another. Then I discovered running, and a whole new world of fitness and endurance opened up for me. In the beginning, I wasn't fast and couldn't run very far. But I kept training and eventually competed in marathons and triathlons. I loved the runner's high and the sense of achievement I felt when crossing a finish line.

Then, after my divorce, a buddy and I took up trail running, covering distances I'd have never thought possible just a few years earlier. Drew and I started with a fifty-kilometer run, then stepped up to fifty miles and even a hundred miles at a time, through some of the country's most beautiful scenery.

Drew and I have trained together for a long time, so when we decided to complete the famous Rim-to-Rim-to-Rim run in the Grand Canyon, we were confident we'd succeed as usual. The course was a "mere" forty-seven miles—from the South Rim down to the Colorado River in the canyon floor, up to the North Rim and back again. That meant a cumulative elevation change of twenty-four thousand feet, but we were sure our extensive training would more than prepare us for it. I added pictures of the canyon to my vision board and dreamed of the day I could cross off the run on my list of goals.

In June 2016, Drew and I descended from the South Rim at 5:00 a.m. on a chilly desert morning. Our plan was to be back where we started by 7:00 p.m. that evening, fourteen grueling but satisfying hours later. It took only three hours for us to fall behind that pace and to suspect we'd grossly miscalculated the magnitude of our undertaking. By noon, the temperature in the canyon was 114 degrees, with an apparent heat index of 140. There was no shade. We made it to the bottom of the canyon, struggling with shooting pain in our legs. Other than a couple of rafters floating down the river, no other people were in sight. Drew and I started the next leg of the journey, up to the North Rim, but by 2:00 p.m. we could no longer deny we were in real trouble. Just three miles from the top, we decided to turn back, knowing we should have done so miles earlier.

We could barely breathe, and we couldn't lower our heart rate, even with resting. Then the vomiting set in. Nothing we ate or drank stayed in our stomach more than a minute. We were suffering from severe heat exhaustion, and muscle cramps kept us from moving at more than a snail's pace. I can honestly say I had never been more afraid for my life. It took nine hours for us to inch our way from the river back to the South Rim. We reached our car at 3:00 a.m., twenty-two hours after we'd left it with such high hopes.

Unbelievably, the physical trauma I suffered that day wasn't the worst part of the ordeal—it was the realization that I had failed. I flew home, feeling defeated. Everyone we'd told about our adventure would know how foolish and shortsighted we had been. I worried that I would come across as a fraud. How could I continue inspiring life-changing confidence in others when mine had been shattered so thoroughly?

ARE YOU BASING YOUR CONFIDENCE ON THE RIGHT THING?

Confidence can make you feel like you can move mountains, or even run them, but the wrong kind of confidence won't take you very far.

Merriam-Webster defines confidence as "the state of being certain."[17] In our coaching business, we like to explain confidence as the authentic expression of having certainty and belief in what you are doing and how you are moving toward your goals. With confidence, you can take bold action. You can move decisively with purpose.

There are three types of confidence: false, conditional, and unconditional.

False confidence: With false confidence, people talk a big game. They describe all the great things they *could* do, but they are full of excuses for why they never actually do them. Then, after the fact, they say, "I should have," "I could have," or "I would have." False confidence can also be seen in negative self-talk. People might have a smile on their face and say, "Oh, things are going fine. Today's a great day." But when they look in the mirror, they feel like a loser who can't get anything right.

Everybody has false confidence at some point. We've all had to "fake it 'til we make it," no matter who we are. But it's the worst place to be, because it's when our confidence is the shakiest.

Conditional confidence: When I (Ron) first ran the Rim-to-Rim-to-Rim, I was the picture of conditional confidence: I had based my self-worth on attaining a particular result.

Most people struggle with this. If you have a big day, a big month, or a big quarter—for example, if you've successfully rolled out a product launch or gotten kudos from your boss on a completing a huge, complicated project—then you might hold your head high and feel good about yourself. But if you have a day, week, or year where you don't hit your sales goals or you don't see the results from your advertising campaign, you might feel "less than."

Conditional confidence is not just seen in the professional world—it's part of life. People often attach their self-worth to getting specific results, including results they can't control. For instance, couples who want to get pregnant will sometimes feel they are less worthy in society's eyes if they cannot conceive. Or people who struggle with their weight may only feel good about themselves if they have reached a certain number on the scale.

Unconditional confidence: If we're going to redefine possible, we must replace our false or conditional confidence with unconditional confidence. At Southwestern Coaching, we've worked with tens of thousands of clients over the years, and in our experience, the most successful people all share unconditional confidence.

Unconditional confidence is the best kind of confidence, because it is based on your beliefs and habits. With unconditional confidence, you are aware that sometimes you'll do well and sometimes you won't. You know that your pain and your struggles are temporary. You understand that if you stay focused on your beliefs and stick to your habits, you will persevere. You just don't quit. And you find that you have faith, which eliminates fear. (We'll talk more about faith in the next chapter.)

But what does it actually *mean* to have unconditional confidence? It means having confidence without conditions—without thinking, "I'll feel confident *if* this happens."

When you have unconditional confidence, you wake up every day focused on your life purpose and mission. You don't worry about what others think of you; instead, you focus on offering grace and love. You operate without conditions, and you treat other people without having an agenda. You are authentic and peaceful, knowing that in this moment you are and have everything you need.

Let's look at three key steps to gaining unconditional confidence.

STEP #1: START BY LETTING GO

When you have unconditional confidence, you let go of things you can't control. Instead, you focus on the three things you *can* control: your attitude, which includes your beliefs and self-talk; your activities or habits; and your schedule.

Your attitude: We've talked a lot about attitude and self-talk in previous chapters. Here, you can use positive self-talk and the affirmations listed at the end of each chapter to create an attitude of unconditional confidence. Your attitude is influenced by the people you surround yourself with—a concept that we discuss in greater detail in chapter 6. If you surround yourself with people who lift you up and believe in your hopes and dreams, your attitude will improve. If you surround yourself with people who are negative and focused on telling you why your hopes and dreams are silly, your outlook will suffer. We love this quote from motivational speaker Zig Ziglar, who often said, "Your attitude, not your aptitude, will determine your altitude."[18]

Your activities: Your activities are the actions you do every hour, every minute, and even every second of the day. Your workout routine is an activity, what you eat is an activity, and what you read is an activity. The people you choose to spend time with or decide to help coach, the number of papers you grade, the amount of emails you answer—these are all activities. Going on a date night, reading a news article, and taking your child or niece/nephew on a bike ride is an activity. The things you do that waste time are also activities, such as the amount of time you spend binge-watching TV, mindlessly scrolling through social media, drinking too much alcohol, or gossiping about your neighbors.

Oftentimes we do things without thinking. To get a handle on what fills your time, make a list of all the activities, both personal and business, that you engage in every single day. Now put a check mark next to the activities you actually have control over. Those activities are the ones that you have influence over and will help you reach your goals by building up unconditional confidence.

Your schedule: Your schedule is also typically within your control. You determine what time you go to bed, what time you wake up, when you return a phone call, and what time you stop working.

When you focus on your schedule, you gain control of your time. In their book *Boundaries*, authors Henry Cloud and John Townsend make the point that if you don't like how others treat your time, it's *your* fault.[19] We agree. Every day, through your actions and attitude, you teach the people around you how to interact with you and whether they should respect your schedule.

When you focus on the things you *can* control, meaning your attitude, your activities, and your schedule, you stop worrying about messing up. You're not concerned about your results. Why? Because you have confidence—*true* confidence—born from knowing that your foundation of beliefs, skills, and habits have prepared you for any situation. You know you are doing your best.

My (Dustin's) wife, Kyah, likens confidence to the metaphor of holding sand on a beach. The people you interact with every day are like grains of sand on a beach. If you hold the sand tightly, you are more attached to whether others like you, want to work with you, or choose to be your friend. The harder you grasp that sand, the more likely it is to slip between your fingers.

But when you hold the sand loosely—when you really don't care what people think, or whether they want to work with you, or if they decide to be your friend—most of the sand remains. People with unconditional confidence don't have their self-worth tied up in getting results, and they don't worry about what other people think. They care less, but they get more.

This idea applies to many situations, whether you're an account executive managing a difficult client, a human resources manager giving a company-wide presentation, or a student studying for a final exam. For example, if you have an upcoming test and you stay up all night to cram, you will become frantic, tired, and overwhelmed, which makes it harder to learn. Whatever facts you manage to retain in that last-minute study session will be offset by how bad you feel when you take the test.

But when you have unconditional confidence, you believe in your abilities, so you plan ahead and give your best effort. You focus on the things you can control, such as not waiting until the last minute to study, ensuring you get enough sleep, and keeping a good perspective. You tell yourself, "I can do this." You make and follow a study plan. You are relaxed, feeling the calmness that comes from having true confidence, and because of that you get a higher score.

STEP #2: GET THE RIGHT PERSPECTIVE

One trait you can develop that promotes unconditional confidence is perspective. When you have perspective, you understand that things are usually not as bad as they sound or as good as they may seem.

Perspective leads to confidence. Let's go back to the studying example. Some people, when faced with an important exam, think, "If I fail this test, people are going to think less of me. I won't be successful, and my GPA/future career will be ruined." Those people have lost perspective. Their confidence is shaky because it's conditional.

When you have the right perspective, however, you can keep your eyes on the big picture. You will most likely pass the test, but if you don't, you know that you'll have more opportunities in the future. One test or one "off day" won't make or break your GPA or career because you have the perspective that you are unstoppable—a perspective that is fueled by consistent activity and positive self-talk.

Here are five ways you can develop the perspective that will help bring you unconditional confidence:

1. Identify your current default perspective.

The first step is to be aware of your current perspective. Is it already positive, or does it need some tweaking?

Perspective matters. We often adopt a specific perspective early in life—for example, believing we are better off tackling problems alone, or that we're not allowed to make mistakes—and we don't check in as adults to determine whether it still works for us. We can also get so caught up in our emotions that we quickly lose sight of perspective.

You have a choice in creating your perspective. To maintain a healthy outlook, we recommend creating perspective anchors. These are times in your life where you developed perspective. For example, did you go through a breakup or divorce, only to realize that your current partner is a much better fit for you? You can look back at this event, learn from your history, and quickly remind yourself that things are going to turn out for the best.

Ask yourself, "Do I have an overall positive 'can do' perspective, or is my outlook negative (what a pessimist might call 'realistic')? What is my perspective toward myself, my significant other, or my job?" When you are aware of your default reaction, you can regain perspective right away.

2. Open your mind to new perspectives.

The second step is to identify other, more positive perspectives. You may need to gather more information or educate yourself to identify and adopt a new perspective. You can do this by spending time with people who have a different point of view, reading books about gaining a positive perspective, or hiring a coach. Traveling outside your comfortable "bubble" or volunteering with people who are less fortunate can also give you a broader perspective, reminding you that your situation might not be as challenging as you'd once thought.

One of the easiest things to do is to simply talk with friends, mentors, and coworkers who have different points of view. Avoid venting with people who already share your perspective, and actively look for opportunities to hear new ideas.

3. Experiment with new perspectives.

The third step is to play with these different perspectives. See what works for you and how that perspective will impact your life.

If your previous perspective was "I'm lazy and not very smart," then you will most likely experience depression and anxiety. Tell yourself something positive instead. Say out loud, "I'm always learning! I'm growing, I'm humble, and I'm a good person."

When you start to see yourself from a new angle, your whole perspective shifts. You will begin to find consistent joy, not circumstantial happiness. And that speaks to unconditional, versus conditional, confidence.

4. Choose the perspective that will serve you best.

Step four is to realize that you have the ability to choose your perspective. If you tend to be negative or "realistic," you can consciously decide to be more positive. You can learn to do that through coaching, reading, self-talk, and being selective about the people you choose to associate with, particularly those who you allow to influence your thinking.

A lot of what we do in our coaching programs is help provide perspective. When you surround yourself with the right people, they can help change your outlook. Check in with people you trust from time to time so that you view events through the right lens. Listen to those people and be open to their feedback.

If you're consistently negative about people or events, you are probably making poor decisions. And that's when you lose confidence. When you begin to see yourself and others differently, you'll begin to build unconditional confidence.

5. Practice these positive perspectives every day.

Finally, the fifth step is to be consistent. The changes you've made need to be sustainable.

For example, you can put on an expensive new shirt and suddenly feel confident. But that's not a good long-term tactic, because tomorrow the shirt will be dirty. It will never be new again. You need sustainable principles to create lasting behavioral change, and these principles can transform you from the inside out.

Changing your perspective takes effort. Start by writing down several things you are going to work on. For example, if you want to build your confidence, list three positive things about yourself at the end of each day. This will reinforce your perspective, because you're paying attention to the things you like about yourself throughout the day.

You can also try visualization. Picture a life where you feel centered, carefree, full of joy. Imagine that when negative or bad things happen to you, you don't overreact; you simply take them in stride. You don't feel like you deserve anything, because you understand that all good things are given to you. You are simply happy to be alive, and you strive to spend your time joyfully serving others. You operate out of a perspective of thankfulness and gratitude. (If you'd like some more concrete tips on how to increase your gratitude, see Appendix B in the back of the book.)

Have regular check-ins to make sure you're sticking with your new perspective. When you're stressed, you might revert back to old habits and ways of thinking. But that's normal. You can get back on track quickly.

As we said, these tasks take work, but the payoff is mind-blowing. The lens through which you view the world will transform, and you will experience positive changes. These changes will actually activate the reward center in your brain,[20] encouraging you to continue your hard work so you can feel those positive emotions again and again.

STEP 3: CREATE CONFIDENCE ANCHORS

Just as you can create perspective anchors, you can also establish confidence anchors.

A confidence anchor is a victory that you can revisit—a memory of a time when you redefined what was possible. For example, you might remember when you broke a personal fitness record, won a baseball game where the odds were stacked against your team, or conquered a fear that was holding you back at work or in your personal life. That event was a turning point, a catalyst in your history that you can trace back to and say, "After this event happened, I changed." When you leverage that event, you can catapult yourself to the next level of belief and confidence in what's possible.

Anchors are solid, strong, and immovable. They stand firm in any storm. Confidence anchors will help you stay calm. They can literally mean the difference between living your life with peace and joy or suffering through the day with stress and anxiety.

What storms did you experience yesterday or even just this morning? Did you open an email that raised your blood pressure or get news that frightened you? We experience storms all day, every day. That's why we need anchors.

Confidence anchors work because they become stepping-stones. Once you've accomplished something, you know that you can accomplish even more. You can create a confidence anchor for yourself or for others. You can provide one for your whole company, giving your team an anchor to reference when times are tough. Or you can set a personal confidence anchor just by doing something new—or even better, doing something that scares you.

One thing to watch out for with confidence anchors is "peaking."

You don't ever want to let yourself think that you are at your peak, or that you've "arrived." Because as soon as you've peaked—everything else is downhill. You want to avoid being like the stereotypical high school quarterback who spends his whole life retelling the same story because those were the glory days.

Instead, use your confidence anchors to catapult you to the next level, where you can then find your next confidence anchor to keep moving forward.

When you leverage confidence anchors, you know that you can keep going because you have the evidence that you can succeed. You are called to do more, serve more, and touch as many people's lives as possible.

Both of us (Dustin and Ron) have used confidence anchors to propel our business and personal lives forward. Here, we've each described the biggest confidence anchors from our past:

1. Dustin's confidence anchor: the advantage of looking back

I (Dustin) have already described two huge confidence anchors in my childhood and early life: getting baptized as a Christian as a thirteen-year-old, and then three years later, winning a wrestling match I was supposed to lose. (This confidence anchor helped me to go all in with other sports, and I went on to get a college scholarship to play NCAA football.) In both cases, I emerged as a different person, transformed spiritually, mentally, and emotionally by the realization that I could be and do more than I had ever thought possible.

Building on these confidence anchors, I developed a third confidence anchor when I broke the all-time sales record for Southwestern Advantage as a twenty-year-old college student. During that year, I sold more books than anyone out of the two hundred thousand people who have worked with Southwestern

Advantage since 1868. If you had asked me years earlier, I'd have scoffed at the idea of accomplishing something that bold. But that's the power of confidence anchors: each new win builds momentum for the next. Of course, every new goal has its own set of challenges that push you to the limit of endurance. That was certainly true for me as a college student working for Southwestern Advantage. I worked many eighty-five-hour weeks, and my first summer I was tempted to quit. During those times, I'd remind myself of what happened that day on the wrestling mat or some other moment when I had given 100 percent. Those confidence anchors helped me to push through the pain and keep selling.

My success at Southwestern Advantage led to another significant confidence anchor as a twenty-two-year-old new college graduate: cofounding Southwestern Consulting, a sales and leadership coaching, speaking, and training business that has grown into a nearly $18 million company with three divisions in just over a decade. At one point in that journey, we were $1 million in debt. But we drew on past confidence anchors and decided not to quit, and over time we became one of the most profitable businesses in Southwestern Family of Companies.

We started off as a motivational sales seminar business called Success Starts Now! None of us had experience as professional speakers—we were a group of post-college kids. We hired a consultant who told us that if we could sell two hundred tickets at $300 apiece during the first five years of business, we'd be competing with big motivational speakers like Brian Tracy and Zig Ziglar.

For our first event we sold seven hundred tickets for $300

each. When people asked who the speakers were, we'd confidently look them in the eye and answer, "We are, of course!"

While we got the business off the ground, I worked at an executive extended-stay hotel, using a bedroom nightstand that doubled as my desk. Some days I didn't bother getting dressed and made a hundred calls a day, cold-pitching people we prospected from the phone book to sell workshop tickets. When people would ask how we planned to pull this off, I'd always give the same answer: "We'll figure it out!"

And we did. We created a program and a script for that first seminar that contained much of the material we still use to this day—in particular, the RAFT technique that helped us mobilize at the beginning of the COVID-19 crisis. (For more details on the RAFT technique, see Appendix A at the end of this book.)

None of that would have been possible without the foundation of previous confidence anchors in my life. Every win sets the stage for the next, and the next.

2. Ron's confidence anchor: completing a major goal

One of my (Ron's) biggest confidence anchors has been my second Rim-to-Rim-to-Rim run. After failing to meet our goal of running the Grand Canyon the first time, you might think my buddy Drew and I would have been hesitant to try again. It's true that my confidence was deeply shaken by how badly we missed the mark. But even before we left the South Rim parking lot that day to head home in defeat, Drew and I looked at each other and said, "We'll be back."

Six months later, in November 2016, we made good on that promise. This time when we got out of the car at 4:00 a.m. on a frosty fall morning and looked over the edge into the canyon below, we were not the same men. For one thing, that previous summer, we had trained differently, building on what we had learned. We ran at higher elevations and in warmer temperatures to acclimate. We educated ourselves about how to work through cramps and manage our body temperature more effectively.

More important, we had shed the ridiculous idea that what lay ahead would be similar to any of the runs we'd done before. Long gone was the cocky notion, "We've got this!" We also stopped defining success by how long it might take to complete the circuit. In other words, we approached the challenge with a very different mindset—and a new kind of confidence.

I'd like to say that made all the difference, and we breezed through the course faster and easier than expected. But I can't. Even without the searing heat of summer beating on us every minute, we still vomited occasionally and had to rest our cramping muscles frequently. It took eighteen hours to arrive back where we started—four hours longer than we'd hoped. Many times through the long day we wondered if we were destined to fail again. But we didn't quit, and ultimately, we finished what we had started that June. This time, when we drove back to the airport, our exhaustion and pain were tempered by joy instead of compounded by defeat.

That's why, of all the confidence anchors I've created in my life, our completion of the Rim-to-Rim-to-Rim run is one of the most memorable and most powerful. In fact, our sense of achievement was that much sweeter for having failed the first time! When you are bold, courageous, and take risks—when you just *go for it* with everything you've got—even "failure" can be a good thing. Allowing an experience to strengthen and refine your confidence can help you bounce back better than before.

WHAT UNCONDITIONAL CONFIDENCE IS *NOT*

We've provided a few practical steps to help you develop unconditional confidence, such as learning to let go, having the right perspective, and creating confidence anchors. Once you've completed these steps, it could be easy to pat yourself on the back. But there's a big difference between confidence and cockiness. Cockiness is confidence taken to the extreme—expecting the best because you believe you *are* the best.

I (Dustin) struggled with this kind of entitled thinking early in my marriage. Entitlement is a toxic state of mind. Anytime I've indulged in thinking that I "deserve" something, bad things have happened to prove me wrong. In fact, that attitude nearly cost me my marriage and my relationship with my daughter, Haven.

After five years of marriage to Kyah, I had become a self-serving jerk. I truly believed I had earned all the good things in my life and deserved to be treated accordingly by my wife. For example, if I worked hard all day, I didn't think I needed to wash the dishes or take out the trash when I got home. I bought season tickets to the Tennessee Titans football games, leaving my wife and daughter alone for many long hours on weekends to go hang out with my friends. I thought I should be able to do what I wanted, when I wanted, and that it was Kyah's job to be grateful for all the material things I had provided like our house, cars, trips, and clothes.

That perspective eventually led me to the darkest year of my life. In response to an unresolved conflict with Kyah, I allowed myself to indulge in behaviors I'm not proud of now—all because I thought I "deserved" certain things. When the day of reckoning finally came, it brought us to the brink of divorce. The divide between us was so deep that even our counselors and pastor advised us to go our separate ways, suggesting to us that some differences can't be resolved. I begged Kyah for forgiveness, but I didn't really know what that meant. We separated and filed the papers for divorce.

Then, after a brief visit with my daughter, Haven, I hit bottom. I was living apart from Haven at the time, so I looked forward to every precious minute we could spend together. One night, she begged, "Daddy, don't leave me!" when I dropped her off at home. Back at my rental apartment, the sound of her cries rang loudly in my ears, and I could finally see the naked truth: Every good thing I had, including my time with Haven, was a gift from God, not my own doing. I didn't deserve any of the credit and certainly was in no position to demand some kind of special status in my relationships. For the first time ever, I truly came to terms with my selfishness. I was broken.

So I surrendered. I let go of it all—including my ego.

I gave up my football season tickets, which I thought were a reward for my hard work but were really just an excuse to spend time away from home. I canceled all work-related travel for four months, including some choice "perks" that I had seen as the fruit of my labor, like an all-expenses-paid dove hunting trip to Argentina on a private jet. I fasted, started running and working out every day, stopped drinking alcohol, and lost forty pounds. I read thirty books in four months and listened to the entire Bible on audio. I purged my soul.

I stopped begging my wife to take me back. I accepted our situation and decided to love her regardless, even if we got divorced. I truly apologized for how much I hurt her. I learned to hold my life loosely, like a handful of precious sand. I could have lost my job. I almost certainly had lost my marriage. However, I was determined that I would *not* lose my soul. I focused on trusting God and not leaning on my own strength and understanding.

Thanks to God's grace, and despite our painful and angry history, Kyah saw these changes and took one more chance. "I see something different in you," she told me one day. "I realize you are working on things, and I want you to know that I am open to working on our marriage too." Together, that's what we did. It has been a daily process of rebuilding and learning to love and honor each other in new ways. But as of this writing, we've been joyfully married for fifteen years. She is the love of my life, and I'm so thankful to be her husband. We still have our struggles, and we definitely do not have it all figured out—but even so, we have been able to help many other couples who are struggling to stay the course, simply by sharing our story.

For me, redefining possible has included changing my entitled thinking. I've learned to rethink how I see myself in relationship to God and others, adopt unconditional confidence, and learn that my sole identity is being a child of Christ. This path has led me through years of pain, suffering, and mistakes—and I'm extremely grateful for it.

POWER STATEMENTS

Here are some affirmations to help you build unconditional confidence:

"I always communicate with confidence and unwavering truth."

"I'm worthy of great things."

"I build other people's self-esteem."

"I'm a leader who raises the confidence of the people on my team."

"I know that failure is temporary and setbacks will only make me stronger."

"I'm a capable, energetic person who has what it takes to succeed."

"I bounce back quickly."

"I've always got the right perspective."

"My potential is sky-high; I'm confident I can succeed."

_____

_____

_____

_____

_____

_____

_____

_____

_____

_____

SPOTLIGHT ON STRATEGY #5:

Kelley McClurkin Cultivates Confidence

The vast majority of our coaching clients at Southwestern Coaching are directly involved in high-volume sales. They usually work in industries like insurance, banking, financial planning, or wholesale goods and services.

So when Kelley McClurkin heard about our coaching program, her first thought was that she didn't qualify. "I'm not a salesperson," she told us. Fortunately, we had the opportunity to help her see how wrong she was about that.

Admittedly, it's easy to understand why Kelley didn't see herself as a candidate for coaching at first. She was the owner of a small business—Bread Kneads Bakery and Deli in Findlay, Ohio. She spent her days making pastries, quiches, specialty breads, and sandwiches for a niche clientele, relying mostly on foot traffic and word-of-mouth marketing.

She was also devoting a lot of time to being what we call a "firefighter." That describes how 99 percent of our coaching clients are operating on day one of the program: they first attack whatever is brightest and hottest at the moment, often neglecting what is "important" to deal with what seems "urgent." This strategy left her convinced she simply didn't have the time for anything else.

But Kelley wanted more out of her business, and she was wise enough to see that attracting whole-sale customers was one powerful way to get it. That meant doing the one thing she had already told us she wasn't capable of: becoming a salesperson. It also meant letting go of her mostly passive and reactive approach to running the bakery and replacing that with systems that were much more focused and intentional. Ultimately, she was more afraid of staying stuck than of leaving her comfort zone.

Over the years at Southwestern Coaching, we have refined the nuts and bolts of how to help a person—or a whole team—meet goals like Kelley's. Our modules help our clients with their visioning; time management; team recruitment, onboarding, training, and retention; perfor-mance metrics; culture-building; and so on. But Kelley's story illustrates the critical importance of one qual-ity that only our clients can provide: they must possess the confidence that they have what it takes to succeed. Everything else depends on this.

Kelley's biggest obstacle was one she had erected herself when she said, "I'm a baker, not a businessper-son." Happily, she proved to be highly coachable. One of our team members started coaching Kelley, and during the course of their work together, she:

- Gained control of her time with focused scheduling and clear boundaries.
- Moved beyond a "minimum wage" hiring mindset to build a team of motivated, like-minded people.
- Reverse-engineered her vision into tangible action items and then made them a daily priority.
- Overcame her fear of selling to people she didn't know and mastered the specific skills needed to do it well.
- Set the goal of landing eight new wholesale contracts—and then surpassed it by securing eleven very strong customers for her products.
- Sold her business in 2019 for far more money than she'd ever dreamed possible before coaching.

Along the way, every fresh win became a new confidence anchor for Kelley—another reason to believe in herself and her vision. Her initial negative self-talk ("I'm just a baker") gave way to a whole list of positive affirmations she used to guide her each day.

After selling Bread Kneads, Kelley set a new goal, one that would have terrified her before redefining what is possible in her life: she decided to find a job in sales.

Fortify Your Faith

*"Faith is permitting ourselves to be seized
by the things we do not see."*
—Martin Luther, leading force in the
Protestant Reformation

L ike many of the strategies that help us to redefine possible, faith can be difficult to describe or define because it's not always tangible. But we believe this strategy is one of the most important elements in achieving personal transformation. In fact, we would go as far as to say that true, meaningful change is possible only when we have faith.

Faith is a key part of both of our lives. Over the years, God has spoken to us in many different ways. When He was trying to reach me (Dustin) as a hard-headed and selfish young person, He repeated himself—*three times.*

I was twenty-one and working as a door-to-door salesperson for Southwestern Advantage. I was driven to sell more products and make more money than anyone else. One day I arrived at a house first thing in the morning, and all thoughts of selling flew out of my mind. Lightning from a thunderstorm the previous night had struck a tree that fell onto a truck in the driveway. What appeared to be a live power line was lying on the ground in the yard. I leapt from my car and rushed to the door to tell the residents what had happened.

I knocked, but the woman who answered didn't seem interested in my warnings about her damaged property. Instead, she invited me inside and handed me a Bible, telling me I was the subject of a dream she'd had the night before. She said God wanted her to tell me that I'd been given a gift and that I was either going to use it for Him or against Him. I was dumbfounded, to say the least.

A few weeks later, in the middle of a sales presentation across town, another customer suddenly looked at me with a strange expression and stopped me mid-pitch. "Hey, I just feel like I need to tell you that you've been given a gift by God," he said. "You can use it for good or you'll use it for evil." These two messengers—who didn't know each other or me—had both said essentially the same thing. I had no idea how to process what I was hearing, so I simply put it out of my mind.

After several months, I was preparing to knock on a door in a different neighborhood when I heard my name: "Dustin! Dustin!" I turned and saw a woman running toward me in slippers and a white bathrobe. When she reached me, out of breath, I recognized her as one of the people I'd spoken with the day before.

"I had a dream about you last night," she said. "I'm supposed to tell you that God has given you a gift, and you're going to use it for Him or against Him."

Later, as I tried to make sense of all this, I asked myself, "What does all of this mean? What am I supposed to do with my life?" The answer was loud and clear in my mind, almost as if I were hearing an audible voice: *help people.* That's all? I was frustrated and wanted to hear more. "What does that mean?" I said out loud. Again, I heard a voice in my head: *help people.*

I stopped and took a hard look at my life to that point. I realized that nothing I'd done, said, or thought about—not a single decision I'd made—had anything to do with helping other people. Being good at sports like wrestling and football had been about winning awards, being popular, and impressing girls. And my job had been about making money, breaking records, and being the best. It was all for me. I was truly a selfish person.

Though it took me years to understand exactly what my gift might be and what it would mean for me to truly help and serve people, I knew one thing for sure: to reach that potential, I had to have faith.

FAITH: WHAT IS IT?

Faith is important to both of us, yet we struggled to write about it at first. *Merriam-Webster* defines faith as a "firm belief in something for which there is no proof; complete trust."[21]

But it's even more than that.

It's acting on an internal conviction. It is trusting in the unknown and the unseen and being willing to step out and act even though you don't know what is going to happen. Faith is that X factor, an intangible quality that makes all the difference when you have it. When you feel stuck or complacent, faith is the elixir. Best of all, faith is enduring. It doesn't fade.

The word *faith* is mentioned hundreds of times in the Bible, the best-selling book of all time.[22] In one of the most famous passages of the New Testament, the apostle Paul pairs faith with hope and love, stating, "Three things will last forever" (1 Corinthians 13:13, NLT). A lot of people put time and effort into love and hope. But rarely do people talk about how to have more faith.

In order to redefine possible, though, you have to have faith.

Nothing great has been done in this world without extraordinary faith. Taking a leap of faith means moving past your doubts or lack of trust and acting on your convictions to start living the life you desire.

Faith works best when aligned with vision, whether that's going after a massive goal, starting a business, or taking a financial risk, such as hiring a coach, going back to school, or selling a house. Every world-shaper throughout history has had an extraordinary amount of faith. Faith is necessary to accomplish big goals. We need to have faith to head into the unknown.

Without faith, we are more likely to give in to fear: We hesitate to reach for big goals because we fear that we won't measure up. We stay stuck because we worry that we won't be able to live up to people's expectations (or even our own).

Without faith, we cannot accomplish anything extraordinary.

FAITH VERSUS FEAR

My (Ron's) wife, Desireé, took a major leap of faith years ago that transformed her professional and personal life. Long before I met her, she faced a heart-wrenching challenge with life-changing implications. When she was a young, single woman working a corporate job in Kirkland, Washington, Desireé discovered she was pregnant. Marrying the father was not an option, and Desireé knew she would have little help.

It caused her to question everything—especially her own beliefs and values. Could she raise the baby and provide financially? Would she choose to, even if the answer was yes? How would this baby change her life and her dreams for her future? She had always hoped to be a stay-at-home mom, but Desireé felt that possibility slipping away. Scared, alone, and confused, she gave birth to a beautiful baby girl and named her Hartley.

Of all the life changes this decision brought about, Desireé was least prepared for how reluctant she would be to part from Hartley during working hours. The thought of leaving her daughter at daycare and enduring long absences seemed excruciating to her. She didn't know how she would do it, but Desireé was determined to find a way to stay home with her daughter.

Around that time, she started making fashionable headbands for Hartley. When more and more people began admiring them— and wanting to know where she'd bought them—an idea took shape. What if her dream of being a stay-at-home mom wasn't gone after all? Could she build a business that allowed her to make a living *and* spend time with her baby at home?

Desireé believed the answer was yes. She had faith in her skills and in her vision of wanting to stay home with Hartley. In a giant leap of faith, she quit her job and moved in with her sister. There, at the kitchen table, Desireé's business, Harts and Pearls, was born. It was a crazy struggle, involving a lot of sacrifice, long hours, and hard work, but within a couple of years, she and Hartley moved into a place of their own. Most years since then, the company has seen double and even triple growth in sales. In 2018, Desireé sold fifteen thousand headbands in a variety of styles, from casual to elegant. After running the entire operation for the first few years, she now employs a team of seamstresses and assistants as well as an army of people to help market her products online, offer them to wholesale distributors, and sell them at craft events around the country.

What set Desireé apart from thousands of other people who remain stuck in fear and want? Faith, and the willingness to act on it.

FAITH VERSUS BELIEF

Faith is often confused with belief. But unlike faith, belief is more concrete and tangible, like having a set of principles. For example, when someone asks you about your beliefs, you might say, "I believe it's important to treat everyone with kindness and respect" or "I believe the most essential ingredient in a marriage is honesty."

If your beliefs are your map, then your faith is your compass. Beliefs are seen in the here and now, in the minutiae of your daily life. Faith, however, is more abstract. It's about trusting that something will happen in the future.

Everyone has faith. On a spiritual level, you have faith in what will happen after you die—whether you are a Christian who believes in heaven or an atheist who believes nothing exists beyond this world. On a business level, you have faith that you're going to achieve your goals, that your company will fulfill its mission, or that the economy will rebound. On a personal level, you have faith that your family and loved ones will be there for you in times of trouble.

Just to be clear, you don't need to participate in a specific religion to have faith. You can have faith in other people, in a company's vision, or in your calling. When you have faith, you're focused on the future you have yet to see.

Gandhi had faith in his ability to create change in the world by organizing nonviolent protests. Alexander the Great had faith in his Macedonian army. Even the German philosopher Friedrich Nietzsche had to have faith in his reasoning to declare that "God is dead."

In the business world, there are many examples of people who have tremendous faith in their goals. The late Steve Jobs, who founded Apple Computer, had faith in how people would act and what kind of lives they would want to live. He knew consumers would want to have the coolest phone or fastest, most interactive laptop. Everything he invented and invested in was about trends and people's emotions. When asked about what spurred him on through low points in his career, Jobs said, "It's not a faith in technology. It's faith in people."[23]

We all should have faith in people. Not everyone may be interested in technology, but everybody is invested in people, whether they're the head of a business, part of a team, or a member of a family. Of course, there's a caveat: if we put *all* of our faith and our hope in people, we will surely experience disappointment. That's why we (Dustin and Ron) both strive to put our faith in God. Unlike people, God has never let us down.

FAITH LIFTERS VERSUS FAITH BUSTERS

Your sense of faith can be affected by the people around you.

Motivational speaker Jim Rohn famously said that you are the sum total of the five people you spend the most time with. We agree. Do those five people have faith? If the people you surround yourself with are negative, or they focus only on what won't work, then they are most likely minimizing your faith. But by spending time with people who have a strong and positive belief system, you can increase your own faith.

One practice is to develop a group of "advisors" or "board of directors" to consult for advice. Find two to five people who are aligned with your principles or spirituality and ask them for advice on a regular basis. In seeking their wise counsel, you'll begin to let go of your own pride and ego.

Your advisors may also be able to see problems that you can't. Having problems doesn't necessarily mean that you are making mistakes, though—only that you needed to learn something from your experience. Your advisors will help you figure out the truth, and you will build a bigger, better, and more impactful life than you ever imagined.

You might think, "Why do I need advisors when I can listen to podcasts or read books for guidance?" Reading books or listening to podcasts may help you get a new perspective on your current situation, but you also need input from real people who know you. Otherwise, you're just floating in whatever direction the wind is taking you. Your advisors—the people who are in alignment with where you want to be—can help you stay the course. They can encourage you to have faith so you don't waver or get off track every time things get difficult.

FAITH AND DISCERNMENT

I (Dustin) learned the value of surrounding myself with people who, like me, wanted to break records. It wasn't until 2005, a few years after that experience of receiving prophetic messages from strangers, that I finally understood what I was supposed to learn from the command to "help people."

It was my last year working for Southwestern Advantage, and I'd already broken the company sales record. A friend named Theo heard of my success and paid his own way from Singapore to shadow me and learn my process. He confided that he wanted to break Southwestern Advantage's record too! In that moment, Theo became my very first coaching client. I taught him every technique and system I had created on the road to my success, and it worked. Theo set a record in his category at Southwestern Advantage.

That summer I had a breakthrough: I realized that coaching and helping Theo reach his goal was by far the most satisfying thing I'd ever done, even more than breaking the record on my own! The question I'd struggled to answer—"What should I do with my life?"—suddenly became crystal clear. I no longer wanted to focus on simply making money or chasing my own ambitions. I wanted to spend the rest of my life helping other people be their very best selves and achieve their goals. This was the God-given gift those three random people had spoken of to me.

Becoming a coach and helping people reach their potential was my destiny. And I realized I wanted to achieve that destiny working for Southwestern Family of Companies, helping the organization in its mission to build purpose-driven people who will impact the world!

You may be reading this book because you're not sure what your own destiny is or because you feel your life is at a crisis point. Maybe your relationship with your partner or roommate is strained, and you don't know how to fix it. Maybe you don't know whether to stay in your career or go back to school. Maybe you're debating whether to start your own business. Is it time to move on to something else, or should you have faith and keep walking along your current path? When you are at that critical juncture, how do you apply faith in deciding what to do next?

The answer is to spend more time contemplating, praying, and listening.

Listening is a skill that very few people have. And discernment is the muscle that comes from listening. Being able to discern what you're called to do or not do—and when you're called to start or stop—is a gift.

Discernment is important because it allows us to determine whether or not we're making the right decision. We can force things to happen that aren't for our own good or other people's good. Sometimes when we get focused and excited about something, we can make it happen because we naturally put in the effort—but that doesn't mean it's the right thing for us to do. When we don't allow events to unfold naturally, we are effectively forcing open a door. In fact, I (Dustin) like to ask myself, "Am I kicking this door open, or is the door just opening before me so I can walk through it?"

If you feel like you have to kick a door open, then maybe that's a signal that you should take a moment to pray, meditate, or listen before moving forward. But if the door is being opened before you, then that could be a sign that you should cross that threshold.

When you really contemplate, pray, and ask for things like clarity and discernment, it's amazing how those prayers get answered. It's usually not in the way you expected or at the time you hoped—sometimes it's the complete opposite—but you end up getting exactly what you need.

To gain clarity, you can create a habit of reading spiritual or sacred texts, self-help books, or biographies of people you admire. You also might listen to podcasts or sermons that inspire you. Seeking the guidance of wise people and reading the Bible or other important books will give you wisdom and insight that can offer a new perspective on your current situation. When you pray or meditate and read, ask yourself, "What is my destiny? What are my core beliefs? Why was I put on this earth?" Praying and seeking wisdom will help you make short-term decisions and will guide the long-term trajectory of your life.

When you align your destiny with what you do every day, you will redefine possible.

HOLDING ON TO FAITH THROUGH HARD TIMES

Having faith is even more important when you experience hardship. When you face a challenge without giving up, you will strengthen your resolve and increase your faith too.

Everyone will face serious challenges sooner or later. If you are alive long enough, life will eventually punch you in the face. Like Mike Tyson said, "Everybody has a plan until they get hit."[24] When you do get hit, your faith—in God, in people, in your mission— will help you stand back up. Your faith will guide your responses and reactions to unexpected challenges and events that disrupt your life plans.

When you know this, you can lean into the challenges ahead of you. You don't need to put on a smile and act like everything's rainbows and butterflies. Instead, you can embrace everything that's hard in life—the grit, the challenges, the news, and the stuff you fear.

Faith can grow with long suffering. When you go through a challenge, struggle with it and wrestle with it, but don't quit. Don't say, "Forget it, I'm just going to give up." You have to defy the quitter in you. Faith requires endurance. A lot of times, faith isn't rewarded quickly. But true faith is not shortsighted; instead, it helps you stick around for the long term.

STRATEGY SIX: FORTIFY YOUR FAITH

We've talked a lot about personal crises from our past, but we have also faced many professional challenges. In the first full year Southwestern Consulting was in business, the company earned more than $1 million in revenue. But years two and three were horrific. By 2008, we were over $1 million in debt. I (Dustin) and my fellow cofounders had to sit down with Henry Bedford, then our CEO, who said, "I don't know if a bomb needs to go off, but something drastic has to happen or this isn't going to work."

It would have been easy to give up, declare bankruptcy, and go find new jobs. After all, we were in the middle of what is now known as the Great Recession. But we had faith in our business. My business partners and I changed everything about our business model and the way we operated. We shut down the seminar business and started coaching, consulting, and speaking. We also altered our compensation plan to be all performance-based.

We rode the roller coaster and stuck it out even though many people doubted us. In 2019, Southwestern Consulting had nearly $17 million in revenue, with the coaching arm of the business bringing in more than 90 percent of the company's revenue.

Then the world shifted for everyone once again with the emergence of COVID-19. But unlike the Great Recession of 2007–2009, this time we were facing both a volatile economy as well as a global health crisis, the likes of which hadn't been seen in one hundred years. Fortunately, our team at Southwestern Consulting had the tools—and faith—to address the crisis head-on. We used the techniques in this book to adapt to the times, and we recalled the lessons we had learned in 2008.

How did we turn the business around? Each time, we had faith in what we did, faith in the people we worked with, and faith in the mission we're on to help people reach their goals. Even though we had to change our business model, our mission—and our faith in it—never wavered. Did we experience a lot of suffering during those uncertain periods? Yes. But it increased our faith in our mission, vision, and value even *more*.

You, too, can rely on your faith when you face trials. The next time you see a challenge coming your way, instead of running from it, try to welcome it as an opportunity to strengthen your faith.

BECOME A FAITH BUILDER

Now that you've read this far, we want to encourage you to watch the world more carefully. It may sound weird, but notice the suffering around you. Pay close attention to the redemption stories. You'll see stories of people overcoming adversity. You'll hear about people renewing their strength. These reports will reaffirm the truth that we as humans were meant to overcome obstacles. Every person who has ever lived has had setbacks, but when you are a man or woman of faith, you can have greater hope.

It can be hard to know what to say to people who are grieving the death of a loved one, dealing with addiction, or trying to revive their once-successful small business. But one thing you can do is acknowledge their faith. You might say, "Your faith has always been so strong, and I know it will sustain you during this time." Or, "I admire your calm and peaceful outlook. I know you'll be able to shine through this." Or, "I have always admired your ability to see the good and to be patient with your circumstances."

By doing so, you're speaking your own faith into other people. When the people around you are fearful, rigid, or full of doubt, your words can give them a dose of hope, strength, and courage—helping them take the leap of faith that they need.

Of course, in order to encourage others with your faith, you first have to extend grace to yourself. Faith and grace are tied together. Grace is a tangible way to show faith.

We've met so many people who are working hard to redefine possible for their lives, but when they reach this stage, they get stuck. They are ashamed of how they handled a conversation or a confrontation at home or work. They're holding grudges for wrong-doings that colleagues, friends, and family committed months and sometimes even years ago. They can't move past their past! They think they are punishing the people who hurt or sidelined them . . . but without realizing it, they're really hurting themselves.

Grudges are the opposite of grace. We have coached count-less people on how to show themselves—and others—grace and how to find freedom in forgiveness as they redefine possible. Once they let go of their "right to be hurt," they begin to shine. They can share their faith with others. They can see things in people that those people don't see in themselves.

If you haven't experienced grace yourself, it's hard to give grace to others. And yet without grace, it's hard to have faith, because grace is the action of faith. What a gift!

∾

This chapter completes another formula:

Belief + confidence = faith.

If you embody faith, you can walk confidently in your beliefs. But it's hard to walk in faith if you're not confident, and it's impossible to live a life of faith if you're not solid in your beliefs.

When fear or uncertainty has a grip on you, faith will bring you freedom and success. If you stay open, try to grow your faith, surround yourself with the right people, and embrace hard lessons, you will find new horizons and opportunities beyond your wildest dreams.

POWER STATEMENTS

To strengthen your faith, try incorporating some of these affirmations into your daily practice:

"I increase the belief, energy, and confidence of every person I meet."

"I empathize with others' struggles, pains, and regrets and help them embrace truth, forgiveness, mercy, and love."

"My mission is to help others reach their greatest potential every day."

"God gives me all strength, courage, and hope."

"I have faith in humanity and believe in the greater good."

"I am a person of faith."

"My faith helps me overcome all obstacles."

"I listen to God and trust His leading."

"I choose to live a life of faith, not fear."

_____

_____

_____

_____

_____

_____

_____

_____

_____

_____

Josh Hudson Learns to Fortify His Faith

Occasionally, people come to Southwestern Consulting seeking help with issues not covered in business school. Because of the nature of their companies, they are struggling, not with time management or hiring practices or lack of long-term vision. These leaders are troubled by a much more common human challenge.

Family.

It can be hard enough to maintain healthy day-to-day relationships among team members who have only their professional lives in common. But when a business is owned and operated by one or more members of a family, the obstacles to success can have roots reaching back decades.

On paper, Josh Hudson was a model of success. When he came to me (Ron) for coaching help, he had an enviable income and shared a good life with his wife and two kids. Josh was the CEO of Hudson's Furniture, a company his father founded in 1981, the year Josh and his twin brother, Adam, were born. He had helped steer the company through an impressive financial turnaround after it nearly cratered during the Great Recession of 2008. Just ten years later, Hudson's

Furniture was named Retailer of the Year by the Home Furnishings Association. The chain boasted eighteen outlets across central Florida and was approaching $100 million in annual sales.

Yet when we started our journey, Josh was not fulfilled. He was putting in long hours and dealing with a lot of conflict at work. He was not sleeping well. He was irritable and depressed. Even more, he was unsure that any of the unhealthy dynamics at work would ever change. Josh was unable to enjoy the fruits of his success because he was stuck in emotional and behavioral patterns with his brother, father, and others in the workplace. These interactions had tainted everything else about his daily experience of life.

"I know I was in danger of being less than my best for my wife and kids," Josh admitted. "And I had begun taking out my frustration on members of my team who had nothing to do with the real problem."

After several sessions and lots of listening to Josh's story, it was easy to see what lay at the core of his struggle: a lack of faith.

I'm not talking about spiritual beliefs but another kind of conviction that keeps most people going in hard times. Josh was beginning to lose faith that his professional life would ever really improve. This desperation had only increased his impulse to exert control and to resist what he perceived as injustice. It was destroying him and harming all his relationships, professional and personal.

Over many months, we worked together to change how Josh saw himself, focusing on restoring his belief that he could take charge of his own experience and improve it. Rather than simply agreeing with Josh that his family dynamics were difficult, I helped him to accept his situation. He soon understood that his circumstances would only change when he had *faith in himself* and in his own ability to improve a very difficult family partnership. I helped Josh realize that after so many years of frustration, he could finally find peace in his work. His vision for himself and for his company would be truly possible if he had enough faith in himself and his ability to make changes.

To help him do that, I shared many tools for emotional self-management to help transform his reactive habits into healthy coping mechanisms. With a lot of hard work, Josh relaxed into a more peaceful and accepting version of himself and was able to develop his new faith: in himself, his company, and his future.

Prepare for Impact

"So leave everything on the court. Leave the
game better than when you found it.
And when it comes time for you to leave, leave a legend."
—Kobe Bryant, basketball icon

Redefining possible isn't just about making a difference in your own life. The strategies in this book are designed for you to transform yourself so that you can then reach out to help others.

One of the most powerful opportunities to make an impact is during times of crisis. Challenges allow people to create impact by offering emotional support, showing up, and helping out in tangible ways, such as through meals, prayers, gift cards, and financial assistance.

When my (Ron's) son Van was diagnosed with leukemia in 2016, I was crushed by a crippling sense of helplessness and failure. After all, it was my job as Van's father to keep him safe and give him a happy, healthy life. Suddenly, up against a mortal enemy, I felt utterly impotent and alone. Fortunately, I didn't feel that way for long. As the Beatles song says, I had "a little help from my friends." In particular, Dustin—and the whole team at Southwestern Consulting—reminded me that I am part of something larger than myself, which had a significant impact on my entire family.

As soon as he heard the news that Van had cancer, Dustin pledged to come see us. That didn't mean a short car ride across town to the hospital, though. I live in Seattle, Washington. I am the only senior partner at Southwestern Consulting working remotely; all other senior leadership works out of our headquarters in Nashville, Tennessee. Despite the distance, within a few weeks Dustin made good on his promise to visit. His presence and encouraging support meant the world to my entire family. He delivered a tangible message in person: *you are not alone.*

That message proved to be far more than just words. Over the coming months, we received invaluable help from the whole team at Southwestern Consulting. The company raised money to help with medical bills and lost income, and team members stepped up to assist with my clients and coaches so that I didn't have to worry about letting anyone down. It was peace of mind and borrowed strength that I desperately needed at the time. My tribe rallied around me and made it possible for me to fully be there for Van and my whole family.

The company's support had a ripple effect, too: it not only impacted our family but also made a difference in the lives of all our team members. At the time, Dustin told me, "Van's situation has affected so many other people beyond his family. It's interesting how God works that way. By making an impact in one person's life, our whole team at Southwestern Consulting grew closer and became stronger for it."

YOU WERE CREATED TO MAKE AN IMPACT

Once you have experienced redefining possible for yourself, you will want to share the process with others.

As you read this chapter, we are going to ask you to think about how you can impact the people around you. But here's the thing: you can't just choose to have an impact and expect to suddenly be making waves. True impact takes time. It should also feel like a calling. You need to be open to the message and be willing to change to truly focus on having a lasting impact.

Ask yourself: "Have I been put on earth to help others? Am I here to lighten their load? Am I here to inspire them? Am I truly present? Do I believe in my purpose? Can I get people fired up about their own mission and goals?" If you answered yes to any of these questions, keep reading for action steps that will help you make an impact on those around you.

Remember, trophies are great and recognition feels wonderful because those are tangible measures of your success—but having something more solid, yet intangible, at the heart of your efforts and actions is better. And that something is the satisfaction that comes when you focus on serving others.

There is a term for the moment when you stop focusing on yourself—letting go of your ego—and start focusing on others first.

In the Bible, the concept is loosely called "dying to yourself." (This concept can be seen in many passages in the New Testament, such as Galatians 2:20, Ephesians 4:22–24, and Philippians 3:8.) This idea is not exclusive to Christianity, though; most of the major world religions encourage selflessness.

It's not easy, but at some point, you need to stop caring about yourself as if you are the most important thing in the world. We're not suggesting that you turn into a martyr. We're recommending that you start focusing on other people and prioritizing their needs.

Once you have done that, your outlook changes. Everything in life becomes sweeter. Things aren't just good, they are great. Living a life in which you have redefined possible takes the mundane of your day-to-day existence and transforms it into a grander picture. I (Ron) like to share the analogy that redefining possible is like driving down the road and suddenly hearing your favorite song come on the radio. Your mood lifts, you start smiling and singing, and you stop worrying about getting to your destination in record time. Once you've redefined possible, your outlook is forever changed. And you can't wait to share it with others.

This outlook doesn't mean that life will be perfect. Your problems don't suddenly go away; you still have tough decisions to make. But you do have shorter valleys and higher peaks. Why? You don't let hard decisions or setbacks hold you back from fulfilling your vision. And you work to help others reach their highest peaks too.

When you clear enough space to hear the call, your potential for making an impact will multiply exponentially.

How do you start? As we've said before, you can meditate, read, pray, or simply pay attention to what inspires you. Maybe you want to try visualizing, thinking, and planning. Or you could choose to go for a walk, get some fresh air, or turn off your phone. Either way, use that time to regain perspective. Quiet time will center you. If your head and heart aren't in the right place, you probably won't be able to make much of an impact.

Once you're ready, you will find many opportunities to influence the lives of those around you. By being authentic and vulnerable, and sharing your struggles and the mistakes you've made, you can help people when they're at a crossroads or dealing with difficulty.

One way to have an impact is to inspire people to keep striving, stay positive, and make the right decisions during difficult times. You can help people accept their circumstances so they are able to move forward (more on this in Appendix A). Another way is to be there for others when they need you the most, such as showing grace and love and mercy to someone who has been condemned or abandoned. You can also help in practical ways . . . just as Dustin and the Southwestern Consulting team did when they supported me (Ron) after my son's leukemia diagnosis.

GET IN THE TRENCHES

One of the best ways you can impact your team at work is to get in the trenches with them. We believe that just as you lead by example, you create an impact by example too.

The first thing you must do is go through the fire yourself. As our mentor Spencer Hays used to say, you can't teach what you don't know, and you can't lead where you won't go. If you want to be a leader, then you actually have to take on the challenge of doing all the hard parts of the job and mastering them first. You must be able to do what you're asking them to do, especially if it's something worthwhile, difficult, and impactful.

That's what it means to lead by example.

Look in the mirror and ask yourself, "Am I actually doing the things I'm asking other people to do?" If you're not doing those hard things, you will feel like—and may be perceived as—a hypocrite.

Impact starts with you.

At Southwestern Consulting, our coaches live and work remotely all across the world. Because we believe so firmly in getting in the trenches as leaders, our team leaders spend time every year shadowing our team members. Whenever possible, we supplement our virtual efforts by going into the field. We see our team member's home office, we watch them do their jobs, and we coach them in person. To become a team leader, you must first qualify through your personal production of selling and coaching over a number of years. Then you earn the right to lead other coaches after personally mastering the skills required first.

The global health crisis of 2020 required Southwestern Consulting to change the way we conducted our business. But even though there were times we couldn't be with our team members in person, we still worked face-to-face as much as possible, doing teleconference calls and having virtual team bonding. We also got creative, ordering pizza to be delivered to each new coach's house so we could enjoy a meal together on video conference.

Why do we make such an effort to be with our team, whether it's onscreen or in the field? Because the impact of a single day together is worth a thousand emails or phone calls. We can't count the number of breakthroughs we've had by investing the time to get on an airplane to spend a day with someone or logging on for a virtual heart-to-heart. It's a memorable experience for us as well as the people we coach. The most authentic conversations happen face-to-face—when we as team leaders show we're willing to see their world.

It also allows us to see things from someone else's perspective when we physically go into their office and house, meet their family, and see how they're organized. We see their computer and their desk, and we see the lens that they're viewing the world through. We've literally gone to people's home offices or visited their homes onscreen, coaching them to set up their office differently or to move their desk to a new area. We've said things like, "Hey, let's put your vision board up. Where's your script? Let's put your goals on the bulletin board."

Showing up for our team members changes their life, it changes their trajectory, and it changes their perspective. By investing our time and showing up on our team members' turf whenever possible, we can help them see their vision clearly so they can focus on making an impact.

Maybe you can't easily hop on a plane. Or maybe you don't

coach a team of people remotely—maybe you see your team members on a regular basis. Whether you work from home or work in the same building as your team, you can still make a huge impact simply by arranging to have lunch or coffee with a coworker or team member. It's hard to overestimate the importance of sitting down off-site (or onscreen, if necessary) and talking about things that matter. Ask about their vision and purpose; find out what they're really here for and why they are doing certain things. In fact, you should be having these discussions every time you talk to a coworker or one of your team members, either in person, on video chat, or by phone.

Why is it so important to keep talking about vision and ask others about theirs every chance you get? Because if you have a big enough vision, you can propel yourself through tedious or time-consuming tasks to make the change you desire—and you can inspire others to do the same. Albert E. N. Gray said in his classic 1940 speech to the life insurance industry that the most successful people create the habit of doing the things that unsuccessful people don't enjoy doing. In our coaching business, we have found this to be true. If you want to help change somebody's perspective, start by helping them realize that what they view as the daily grind is actually something they need to fall in love with doing in order to achieve their ultimate vision.

That's a big perspective shift. Most people are so focused on themselves that the only lens they can see through is their own selfish thoughts, desires, and outcomes. And it's all driven by ego.

A lot of people spend a mind-boggling amount of time

worrying about what other people think. People tend to fixate on how they look, whether they sound smart or funny, and what other people say about them—so much so that it completely paralyzes their ability to live a full life. You can help your family, friends, and colleagues realize it doesn't matter what other people think, though. All that matters is who they are and what they do.

That shift in perspective will completely change their life.

Recently, I (Ron) was explaining the relationship between impact and redefining possible to a teammate. It finally clicked for her when I described the opposite effect of not taking action, not having a vision, and not wanting to make an impact. "The opposite of impact," I explained to her, "is insignificance. It's having a full bank account but an empty soul. It's having focus, confidence, and drive but not using those qualities for good. All the accolades in the world won't bring love and connection. Impact is the way I want to live. It's the legacy I want to leave with my family."

WATCH FOR THE RIPPLE EFFECT

Many of us like solid results, and uncertainty frustrates us. Although we might be able to count thank-you cards and compliments, we find it hard to figure out how to measure impact.

When thinking about how to quantify the impact you're making, remember that it is complicated. You might make an impact by having excellent principles and being a model of service. Or you may help one person who was ready to quit his or her business, marriage, or even life. That act can be worth as much as helping millions of people with smaller problems.

I (Dustin) was able to do this awhile back during a coaching session. I noticed that my coaching client was visibly distraught. He confided that the next morning, he and his wife were going to file for divorce, and he would take full custody of their kids. He had decided that right after our meeting, he was going to make some risky choices that could potentially ruin his life. I took a deep breath, said a quick prayer, and shared my own past marital struggles with him, explaining how God had brought me from the brink of despair and helped me redefine possible for my own life and marriage. By the end of the conversation, we were both crying and he had changed his mind. Instead of going to a hotel, he went to church. The last I heard from him, he and his wife were still married and committed to working on their relationship.

This ripple effect of impact on one client's life is exactly what we're talking about—the individual touchpoints we can have in several areas of life.

Impact can be created in a variety of different ways. It might be as simple as taking the time to listen to someone in need. Or it might look like helping someone who isn't living by the right principles, is drifting, lacks a vision and mission for their life, or is just being reactive, not proactive. Your impact will be evident when you help them find clarity, have a vision, or live by the right principles, ultimately changing their life in a positive way.

You create an impact when you lead by example, show others the right way to live, and help other people rather than focus on yourself. When you follow the strategies in this book, making them the basis for how you live your life, you change your lens.

Your focus becomes about what you give and how you help others.

We've been leaders in the workplace for many years, and we know this is true: when you are really helping others for the right reasons and have your heart in the right place, people will thank you and tell you that you've made an impact in their life. They'll tell you about their transformations.

It's a cycle. You help people, then they help other people, and then they help other people, multiplying the effect.

One person can have a tremendous impact. For example, take a single coach working at Southwestern Coaching, the one-on-one coaching business that is part of Southwestern Consulting. We work directly with more than one hundred coaches worldwide. Each coach has thirty clients on average, so that's over three thousand clients reached per year. Those clients are growing in life—in their financials, in how they use their time, and in their purpose—which impacts their family members, coworkers, friends, and neighbors. And that's just one coach living out his or her vision of helping others achieve their goals.

Recently, my (Ron's) son P. K. surprised me while I was driving him home. "Dad," he said nonchalantly, "you're not like my friends' dads." I asked him why he thought that, and his response floored me. "Well, you just seem to act differently than they do," he replied. "You're always talking about how much you love your job and you've shared stories of how people you work with live great lives. My friends' dads don't love their jobs. I'm glad you're my dad and that you're helping people." I almost had to pull over to get the tears out of my eyes! There's no trophy in the world big enough that would make me feel happier than hearing that my son could see the difference I was making in other people's lives.

MAKE IMPACT YOUR LEGACY

As we've said, impact is mostly intangible.

We aren't Bill and Melinda Gates or Warren Buffett, who can make a big impact because they can donate billions of dollars to various causes. But just because we can't give billions of dollars to charity doesn't mean we can't have just as much of an impact on the people we meet every day. In fact, impact has little to do with money or financial goals. I (Dustin) often say, "At the end of our lives, God will not care how much money is in our bank accounts. However, we believe you get to look back at the impact you've made in people's lives."

Perhaps the ultimate measuring stick for impact is how many people show up to your funeral. This occurred to me (Dustin) when attending the memorial service of one of my mentors, Spencer Hays, and seeing how much of an impact he made in the lives of thousands of people worldwide. Not only was his memorial standing room only in one of the largest churches in Nashville, Tennessee, it was viewed by hundreds of people online all across the world. Powerful leaders got up one by one to tell some of the most amazing stories about Spencer and the influence he had on their life. I realized that even through Spencer was one of the wealthiest people I had ever known, his real treasure was the way he had reached so many people, ultimately leaving a lasting legacy.

We believe that effecting positive change in people's lives is literally the most rewarding thing you can do. Scientist, naturalist, and humanitarian Dr. Jane Goodall is often quoted as saying, "You cannot get through a single day without having an impact on the world around you. What you do makes a difference, and you have to decide what kind of difference you want to make."[25]

We may not become household names like Oprah Winfrey, Bono, Malala Yousafzai, or Michael Jordan, but we can make an impact on our own household, which will in turn change our communities, workplaces, and beyond. In the end, if we can teach our children how to redefine possible for their lives, and they in turn teach it to their children, and so on, that is the greatest legacy and lineage we could ask for. We hope that, like Spencer Hays, at the end of our lives, people will be lined up at our funerals to share stories of how we positively impacted them and others.

You now, at your fingertips, have the greatest formula to change your life. The seven strategies we've shared are like ingredients for your favorite recipe. To get the results you want, you'll need to follow the recipe order and make sure you didn't forget anything. It's a lot of hard work, but when you stay consistent and follow through, the yield will be incredibly fruitful.

The unbridled joy you'll get after redefining possible, plus the peace you'll have in knowing that you've done all you can to transform your life, means that your life can have an effect that ripples throughout generations.

Your impact can be your legacy, helping you to redefine possible.

POWER STATEMENTS

As you get ready to redefine possible, focus on the idea of impact and the connections we have made in this chapter. Here are some affirmations to keep these ideas at the top of your mind.

"I'm going to keep doing the right thing and focus on impact."

"Money comes and goes, but my impact on someone's life lasts forever."

"I positively impact every person I see."

"I use my time and resources to help others in any way I can."

"I help people reach their goals in life."

"My impact is my legacy."

"I'm the light for the people around me."

"I can change the world with small acts of kindness."

"My smile/listening skills/hospitality/compassion creates an impact."

_____

_____

_____

_____

_____

_____

_____

SPOTLIGHT ON STRATEGY #7:

Nolan Pattee Prepares for Impact

When Nolan Pattee heard about Southwestern Consulting, he was already a successful insurance agent and financial advisor running his own agency for Bankers Life Insurance Company. He had a comfortable six-figure income and had grown his agency to a team of twenty people.

Nolan wanted more, though. When I (Dustin) became his coach, his business was not yet among the top one hundred agencies in the Bankers Life network, but he was determined to reach the top fifty. He also wanted to grow his personal income to $400,000 a year. It was what is commonly called a "big, hairy audacious goal."

One immediate obstacle he faced was the challenge of keeping tabs on offices in eight locations. Remote management is never easy, but Nolan seemed especially vulnerable to taking things personally when thorny issues arose. Those constant mental and emotional distractions threw off his ability to focus on what was important to the business as a whole.

In time, he would adopt the techniques we gave him for streamlining communications and accountability. Yet this would prove to be a relatively easy fix in comparison to the real challenge: Nolan's vision for himself and his company was entirely one-dimensional. For him, it was all about the money and winning.

That single-minded goal dominated Nolan's decisions—including how he went about recruiting, onboarding, training, and retaining team members. He looked only for people who shared his financial goals and assumed that, so long as everyone was making money, nothing else mattered.

He admitted that this attitude wasn't serving him very well when I pointed out the obvious: this prevented others from reaching their own goals. Something needed to change.

There is nothing wrong with seeking financial reward. The problems arise when making money becomes the *only* reason for investing so much time and effort into a business. That's because, as much as we need it to survive, money will only make us so happy.[26] In fact, it is actually one of the flimsiest possible answers we can get when seeking to define a person's *why*. Many well-meaning people have learned that it often feels hollow and unfulfilling to reach purely financial goals; paradoxically, it can weaken a person's motivation to go on.

To help Nolan see this, I insisted he create a vision board—a visual representation of what he wanted to

achieve with his success. At first, Nolan was reluctant to commit the time and energy to create a proper
vision board. But in the end, he relented—and it
completely transformed his approach to business and
life. He learned his previous vision had failed to include
anything that would fit under the most important *why*
of all: to make a positive impact on others.

Nolan quickly saw that what he really wanted was
to be present in the lives of his kids, to take them on
adventurous trips, and to make it to all of their sports
meets. He wanted to build meaningful relationships with
the people on his team. "I never really spent time with
them before," he said. "Now I get to work with friends,
not just employees."

His personal awakening was so transformative that
he paid for everyone on his team to learn how to create
their own vision board. Today he devotes a significant amount of time and resources to maintaining a
company culture that values more than just money.

Not surprisingly, that hasn't stopped him from
meeting his financial goals. Within five years of setting
his first "audacious" goal, Nolan's agency was among
the top ten in the company. His personal income
topped $700,000, and his team grew from twenty
people to more than eighty. Yet more important, he was
able to realize his dream of buying a farm where he can

take time off to spend with his wife and four children. Nolan and his family have also been able to travel the world, making family memories and creating a lifelong impact on his children. At the end of the day, Nolan has redefined possible for himself and his family and has impacted his team and those around him, leaving a legacy that will last forever.

Possible Doesn't Happen Alone

C lose your eyes. Listen to your heart. It's time for you to rede-fine possible.

We are excited to get to the end of this book. We have shared many ideas on how to redefine possible, and now we'd like to draw a few final connections between some of the concepts we have explored.

We have taken you on a journey from focus, ownership, and vision to belief, confidence, and faith—and then finally, to impact. At the beginning of this journey, you might have had one defini-tion of the word *possible*. But now that you've reached this stage and you have redefined possible for yourself, you can see that *everything* is possible, no matter what your circumstances are.

Once all the pieces come together, you will find that you actu-ally feel calmer—more serene and peaceful. By fully letting go of all the stress, clutter, and need for control, you will be able to just be present. Happiness is fleeting, but you will have joy that lasts. Rather than feeling pleasure momentarily and then falling into complacency, you will find a deeper sense of contentment.

True joy and peace are yours to have.

The first formula we shared with you involved the topics in chapters 1 through 3—focus and ownership combine as vision. (Focus + ownership = vision.) In the second formula, covered in chapters 4 through 6, belief and confidence combine as faith. (Belief + confidence = faith.) When you take the end results— vision, faith, and impact (chapter 7)—you'll see that they allow you to reach your whole goal: redefining possible. When your vision, faith, and impact are strong, it changes everything.

You have a calling, which is your **vision**, to motivate you to follow through and master all of the details of what you hope to achieve. You have resilience, hope, and a heart to serve, which is **faith** at its strongest. And you have **impact**, which is drawing people to you and inspiring and guiding your team, family, friends, neighbors, and coworkers with the big and small things you do each day. You know that at the end of the day you can have all the money, devices, and trophies in the world, but they won't give you one lick of joy without making a true impact.

From there, nothing will hold you back.

This freedom is exhilarating. How many times have you been told "No" or "You can't go there" or "You can't do that"? Pretty much since the day you were born, right? When you were young, you didn't understand, but now you know better than to listen to limiting statements. Now you've learned to gain freedom through redefining what really is possible. Instead of feeling gripped by limits, you will feel the freedom of your strong and innovative ways.

A global advertising campaign featuring Muhammad Ali and other famous athletes once asserted, "Impossible is not a fact." We agree with this concept: What one person calls "impossible" is just his or her opinion. Impossible odds create potential, impossible situations are temporary, and impossible circumstances are only what you make them. In fact, like the ad famously stated, the word *impossible* is not even a declaration.

Instead, it's a dare.

YOUR DAILY WORK: THANK, ASK, SURRENDER

Redefining possible will require a commitment you'll need to renew daily. It's like exercise or eating healthy—something you have to do consistently to see results. Otherwise, if you don't keep up the work, you could easily slip back into your more selfish, less-motivated ways.

The shape this work will take is up to you. If you are someone who prays, you can recite a daily prayer of gratitude for everything you have been given. As the stories we've shared in this book show, we believe that all the good things we have were given to us—and none of these gifts is something we deserve. So we should be over-the-top thankful for every blessing we have.

You'll also have to know how to ask for help if you're going on a spiritual journey. You can say, "Hey, I can't do this without you, God." Beyond that, you need to know specifically what to ask for—whatever you're lacking. What are you looking for? Wisdom, discernment, confidence, powerful thoughts, the ability to have hard conversations?

Some of us need to consistently ask for forgiveness for pride and selfishness. No matter how good you get at this, your pride and selfishness may still be there, whether you like it or not. Ego is a dragon that you may have to slay every day. The enemy is the ego, and the battle is for your mind.

Even as you get specific in asking for help, you must also realize that this isn't something you can will to happen. In fact—and this is probably completely different from what you may have read in other self-help books—if you think you can just will these changes into existence, that's a sign that you're in the danger zone. If you try to force things to happen, then you'll typically get the opposite of what you want because you're not doing the hard work to achieve it. You can't just whip up and "positive think" your way into redefining possible.

Instead, take whatever it is you feel you need and want—whatever you're trying to will to happen—and submit it to God or to a higher power. Don't forget to hold those grains of sand loosely. As you submit spiritually, you are allowing for what's meant to be. When you do this, you are saying, "If this is supposed to happen, let the door open, and I'll walk through it. That'll be my sign. And if this is not supposed to happen, if this is not the path that I should have in front of me, then I'm fine with that, too. I'm fine with whatever direction I am being led. I'm going to be ready, I'm going to prepare myself, and I'm going to be open to the opportunity."

What you should be left with is a feeling of peace, a quiet certainty that cannot be found any other way. When you develop the qualities we've discussed—when you really have faith and the kind of confidence, personal vision, and impact we talk about—everything is exactly as it should be.

REDEFINING POSSIBLE MAKES *ANYTHING* POSSIBLE

We don't want to leave you with the impression that we have this all figured out. We are not a perfect example to be held up. Instead, we have a vision for the future, and we work to redefine possible in our own life, every single day.

When we enroll a new client with Southwestern Coaching, we call this enrollment a "life impacted" or a "life changed." My (Ron's) goal at the company is to help as many people as possible transform their lives. So I often ask myself, "Can one person enroll more clients than anyone ever has in the history of the company? Can one person recruit and lead more effectively than anyone ever has in the company?" That's the trifecta—the three parts of Southwestern Coaching.

But that's only one part of my life. In my personal life, I have other goals.

For example, I have challenged myself to get to a fitness spot I've never been before while still having my evenings and weekends to focus on my family and truly be present. I've involved my family in this aspiration, and I am allowing my spiritual life to guide me and be at the true center of it all. I'm getting to the point where I see what life looks like as I'm redefining possible in the present and the future, rather than focusing on what I've done in the past. I always tell groups in workshops I lead, "I'm no different than anyone in this room. I'm just trying to be a little better today than I was yesterday."

DON'T BE A LONE RANGER

As you can imagine, it's a lot of work to maintain all of these attributes and feel motivated to redefine your boundaries. But you don't have to do this alone. We all need help.

We've talked about prayer and submitting to God or a higher power, but you can also seek help by hiring a coach. We firmly believe that everyone can grow from coaching, whether they're elite athletes or businesspeople.

We can all draw strength from each other. We can all find value in bouncing ideas off someone else, regaining perspective, and having someone help keep us accountable. We encourage you to find friends and mentors, even bosses, who are willing to give you honest feedback.

But finding someone who is dedicated to helping you become your best self is the best gift. Working with a coach can put you on a fast track to accomplishing your goals. The right type of coach will customize a plan for you and your situation. Coaches are trained not to talk *at* you, but to listen *to* you. Coaches seek to understand what you're already doing well, identify where gaps exist, and confirm where you can use some support. And when you combine coaching with taking the steps to redefine possible, you'll have a really clear vision—short-term and long-term—of where you want to go.

If you are a longtime leader, executive, or mentor yourself, don't assume that you don't need coaching. In fact, you may need it more than anyone else, because you have the greatest opportunity to impact the most people. At Southwestern Coaching, we match our coaches to clients based on personality, and we can often accommodate requests about spirituality, gender, and in some cases, language. As this book goes to print, we have clients in thirty-five different countries and over one hundred certified Southwestern Consulting coaches. Our coaches have reached more than fourteen thousand clients—increasing their clients' sales on average by 25 percent.

If you want to explore working with one of our life-changing coaches, feel free to contact us at www.southwesterncoaching.com or www.redefiningpossible.com. In addition to offering personal, life-changing coaching, Southwestern Consulting provides a wealth of practical tips and information to its clients. We've included a small portion of this material in two appendices in the back of the book to help you in your journey to redefine possible.

THE HIGHEST CALLING

We want to wish you all the best. And we each want to leave you with a message:

From Dustin

Helping other people is the highest calling you can have. Take the first step of looking into the mirror and start the process of finding your vision, focus, and beliefs. Find joy in everything you do. Be serious about your work and the principles you live by, but don't take yourself too seriously. Life is too short not to have fun. And don't forget to hold life like it's a handful of precious sand. Hold it loosely, with love and grace. First decide what your passion and purpose is, and then give 100 percent. Don't ever give up.

From Ron

When you wake up every morning, renew your commitment to serving others instead of yourself. Challenges will come every day, fear will grip you, and shame and guilt will be a threat, but know that you can overcome your trials. Please live courageously and in peace, knowing that you can and will achieve your highest calling by serving others and lifting them up.

჻

Thank you for taking this journey with us. We think of you reading this book and opening up your mind to our ideas . . . and we are grateful.

You've now got the strategies you need to redefine possible. There are no limits, not even the heavens! Embrace your soul, get ready for hard work, and then go live courageously.

The shattering of normal, the crushing of impossible, and the power of redefining possible begin now.

The RAFT™ Technique

We developed the RAFT technique to combat the tendency we all have to make excuses when things get hard in life.

As you redefine possible, you can use RAFT to encourage yourself to hold strong to your vision and your goals when life throws obstacles in your way. Be empowered to overcome all kinds of adversity with this technique!

A STRATEGY FOR DEALING WITH
THE UNEXPECTED

Everyone has an excuse for why they cannot redefine possible and achieve their potential. We sure have had excuses as well.

Excuses come in different shapes and sizes. A lot of times your excuse for holding back is very real and difficult, such as the death of a loved one, a divorce, or a serious health challenge. Other excuses, however, may be less significant. These can simply be due to a lack of self-confidence or caused by uncontrollable external circumstances like the economy, the weather, the region you live in, industry regulations, or your family situation.

One of our mentors, billionaire Spencer Hays, always said, "There are two types of people in this world: one finds an excuse, the other finds a way. It doesn't take guts, gumption, or determination to find an excuse. Anybody can locate one. It takes quality people to find a way over, under, around, or right through any obstacle that stands in their way."

You may be worried that you are going to be left paralyzed by the pain that comes with change. But we are not going to leave you behind—we're going to offer you a life raft. RAFT is a technique you can use to get unstuck when you are overwhelmed by life's challenging circumstances. This technique can help with adversity of all kinds, big and small. When you remember to apply the RAFT technique, you will empower yourself to overcome obstacles quickly and never make an excuse again.

Let's look at the breakdown of the acronym RAFT:

R: Realize an event is happening to you.

This first step is incredibly important: awareness. You have to be aware that a difficult event is occurring, rather than ignore the situation or your feelings about it.

You'll know an event is happening to you when you notice that you are slowing down in your progress or making excuses about your lack of achievement. This affects your plan, pushing your goals "off schedule." That is your event. Events can be big (like a death or divorce) or small (like car problems or a specific work challenge).

Once you realize something is getting you off schedule and you've identified your event, you are ready for the next step: acceptance.

A: Accept that the event is occurring.

It can be challenging to accept reality. Most people naturally resist accepting events that happen to them, especially if the situation feels extreme and unfair. As I (Ron) often say, "It is my resistance to 'what is' that causes my suffering in life."

It can be difficult to accept when trials happen to you, because typically the event makes for a great excuse. Everyone loves a good dramatic story, and often, when you tell other people about it, everyone around you will agree with how horrible your situation is. Then they might encourage you to relax, quit, ignore the situation, or do whatever is necessary to avoid the pain.

You can try to fight the situation by staying busy or ignore it by numbing your pain with things like food, drinking, shopping, or exercise. You can even pay thousands of dollars and spend months in therapy. But no matter how you choose to handle the crisis, you eventually must come to terms with your situation and accept that the event happened to you.

F: Focus on what you can control.

You can control just three things in life: your attitude, your schedule, and your activity or actions.

Your attitude is a choice. You choose your attitude every day when you wake up in the morning. If you're in a bad mood—congratulations, it's your fault! If you're in a good mood—congratulations, that's your doing too! Throughout history, people have told stories about being in horrible situations—even being in concentration camps or sentenced to death[27]—but they still found joy in something each day. It *is* possible to choose joy.

Your schedule is a choice. You determine what time you wake up and when you go to bed. You control your schedule and your time—and even how people communicate with you. You have the same number of minutes available today as anyone else. Playing the "I don't have time" game is self-sabotage. Again, if you don't like how your schedule and your life looks—congratulations! It's your fault.

Your activity (or action) is a choice. You control the activities you decide to take on every day: how many calls you make; your lack (or excess) of social time; what you do or don't read, watch, and listen to; and—of course—whether or not you make it to the gym. You can decide how much time you want to spend on each of these different tasks. Your schedule is within your control—from the moment you wake up until you close your eyes to go to sleep at night. You set the boundaries around your time.

When you take responsibility and focus on what you can control and stop making excuses about events that happen to you, you can begin to create your own normal and redefine possible.

T: Transform the negative event into positive momentum.

What do Michael Jordan, Serena Williams, and Brett Favre have in common? Besides the fact that they're each one of the all-time best players in their respective sports, they all transformed negative events into positive momentum.

Brett Favre played one of the best football games of his life the day after his dad died, and he led his team to victory in the NFC North Division title that year. Michael Jordan was suffering from extreme flu-like symptoms in game five of the 1997 NBA Finals, and he still performed one of his most significant games ever. He led his team in the win over the Utah Jazz to take the series 3–2. Serena Williams suffered a life-threatening pulmonary embolism in 2011, forcing her off the tennis courts for nearly a year. She came back from her health crisis by winning her fifth singles title at Wimbledon and earning a gold medal in the singles event at the 2012 London Summer Olympics.

GROWTH AFTER TRAUMA

RAFT is a technique we coined that embraces a concept called post-traumatic growth, or PTG. Experiencing personal growth after trauma can completely change your life. When you harness your emotions from a negative event and transform them to create positive momentum, you can break through to a whole new level that wouldn't have been otherwise possible. What was once a negative event can become a powerful tool for growth. An incredible transformation takes place when a person embraces adversity and uses it as fuel to perform.

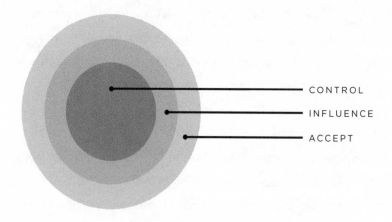

Realizing these traumatic events happened to you, accepting them, focusing on what you can control, and transforming the traumatic event into positive momentum can be the very thing you need to redefine possible and take your life to the next level.

APPENDIX B

Gratitude

G ratitude is not a specific strategy we have in the main text of the book, but it is a very important element in the journey to redefining possible.

We have spent countless hours working with our coaching clients on having an attitude of gratitude. Gratitude is something we also work on every day. It's easy to get caught up in waiting for something better to come along and stressing about "what if," but slowing down and reflecting on what you have can help bring clarity to your vision and your goal to impact others as you redefine possible.

Gratitude takes redefining possible to the next level. In this appendix, we share some additional tips on gratitude and include a space for you to write out things you appreciate.

GRATEFULNESS

Being grateful is different from having a positive attitude. Having an optimistic outlook doesn't necessarily mean you are grateful for your current situation. As soon as we get in the mindset that we "deserve" things, we are in the trap of believing we don't have enough. Anything good is a gift. It's impossible to feel grateful if we feel entitled. It's important to remember that we're on this earth to serve people. Looking for people we can serve every day will help remind us to live out an attitude of gratitude.

Keeping a daily gratitude journal can help keep us on track. When we're in neutral, it is easy to slip into a negative mood or attitude. If we remind ourselves every day what we have to be thankful for, it will help boost a constant attitude of gratitude.

COMPARISON IS THE THIEF OF JOY

Comparison causes stress, frustration, and ultimately limits people's beliefs in what they think is possible.

It takes an extreme amount of self-control and mental toughness not to compare yourself to other people. Think about it. When was the last time you had any of the following thoughts?

- "I would be doing much better if I had Mary's territory."
- "I'm doing more work than Henry, and he needs to pick up the pace."
- "The only reason John is successful is that he gets special treatment by the boss."
- "It's not fair that Sue is getting paid as much as she is. I work just as hard, if not harder, than her."

- "Nancy's marriage seems so much happier than my marriage."

The hardest part of not comparing yourself to other people is the fact that we, as humans, are hardwired to desire what we don't have. Have you ever witnessed a toddler walk up to another child and just take the toy they have? Being content with your current situation can be a challenge.

While competitiveness and wanting to win is a good quality, being too competitive with other people can end up being destructive. It's okay if your goal is to be number one because you think being number one is your potential. It's not okay if your goal to be number one is because you cannot stand the person who's currently number one and you just want to beat them. When people are too competitive with others, they tend to be territorial, selfish, and frustrated that they can't control what other people are doing.

We are called to live up to the potential that we have been given. Our ambitions should come from being motivated to do our dead-level best every day. If our goal is to beat our personal best performance every day, then there would be no limit to what we can do!

Having gratitude can help you avoid comparing yourself to other people. It can also enable you to be content with what you have and break your own belief barriers of what you think is possible.

We often share this poem with our coaching clients, because it powerfully describes the importance of gratitude.

A Beginning of a New Day

This is the beginning of a new day.
God has given me this day to use as I will.

I can waste it or use it for good.
What I do today is important, because
I'm exchanging a day of my life for it.

When tomorrow comes, this day will be gone forever,
leaving something I have traded for it.

I want it to be gain, not loss;
good, not evil; success, not failure;
in order that I shall not regret the price I paid for it.
—Heartsill Wilson

(Legendary football coach Paul "Bear" Bryant famously carried this prayer with him in his wallet.)

Create a Gratitude List

On the following page, make a list of 20 things that you love about your life. Looking at this list every day will reinforce your attitude of gratitude as you redefine possible for your life.

GRATITUDE LIST: 20 THINGS I LOVE ABOUT MY LIFE

1. _____
2. _____
3. _____
4. _____
5. _____
6. _____
7. _____
8. _____
9. _____
10. _____
11. _____
12. _____
13. _____
14. _____
15. _____
16. _____
17. _____
18. _____
19. _____
20. _____

The Power of Self-Talk

A t the end of each chapter, we shared positive affirmations for you to say out loud or write out and post where you can see them daily.

Seeing and saying positive affirmations can change the wiring in our brains to think more positively. This is the power of self-talk. In this appendix, we share even more great techniques for developing your self-talk. It is one of the best things you can do to help achieve your goals.

WHY DOES SELF-TALK MATTER?

There is a great book on self-talk by Shad Helmstetter titled *What to Say When You Talk to Your Self*. The book includes five major premises to improving our self-talk. It says:

- Success results from our actions.
- Actions are filtered by our feelings.
- Feelings are based on our attitudes.
- Attitudes come from our beliefs.
- Beliefs are purely programming.

Self-Confidence Cycle

We are being programmed every day whether we like it or not. We are programmed by the media, other people and outside influences. The decision is yours whether or not you choose to let yourself be programmed by society or choose to program yourself by using positive self-talk.

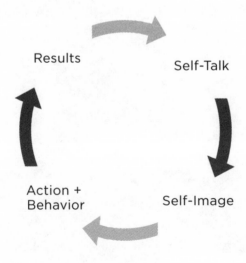

POSITIVE SELF-TALK: THE POWER OF POSITIVE AFFIRMATIONS

> *"Self-talk is defined as what you say about yourself
> to yourself, and what you allow others to say about you,
> that you believe."*

There is a misconception that being positive is what having positive self-talk is all about. Self-talk has nothing to do with being a positive person. It has everything to do with looking in the mirror and honestly saying what you think about yourself.

Your self-talk is perhaps the most important thing in your life. The core of your self-talk is your belief system. Your beliefs construct your attitudes. Your attitudes determine your actions. Your actions come from your feelings. Your feelings come from your self-talk.

Below are some examples of affirmations that specifically relate to confidence.

- *Independence:* "I never have to be told what to do."
- *Execution:* "I actually do what I already know."
- *Studious:* "I am always eager to learn and never feel like I have arrived."
- *Coachable:* "I always work efficiently and follow the system."
- *Accountable:* "I never make excuses!" (e.g., I would have, but . . .)
- *Implement:* "I always use the notes I take."

- *Disciplined:* "I am always aware of the importance of my schedule."
- *Loyal:* "I support my teammates at whatever cost."
- *Objective:* "I remember to criticize or give feedback on the action and not the person, in private and not in public."
- *Determined:* "I can, I will, I'm going to . . ."

If someone stuck a recorder inside your brain over the past 24 hours, we are sure you would agree that the things you tell yourself about yourself would be scary. Most people spend their entire lives telling themselves what they can and cannot do.

> *"The key to success is having amazing self-talk."*
> —Spencer Hays

Your self-image is directly tied to your self-talk. When you look in the mirror, do you see someone who is fat, ugly, dumb, a failure, a bad husband/wife, a lousy father/mother, a victim, a martyr, a jerk, a nag, a mediocre worker . . . or do you see someone who is fit, sexy, smart, a winner, the world's best husband/wife and father/mother—someone who will go over, under, around, or straight through any obstacle in their way? As humans, we are programmed to think a certain way, whether we like it or not. Either you choose to give up control of your own programming and let the media, society, or your friends and family program you with what you believe about yourself and the world, or you take control of your self-talk and start programming yourself with the things you want to believe about yourself and the world.

HOW TO WRITE GREAT AFFIRMATIONS

A simple way to change your life is to take what was previously a weakness or growth area and write an affirmation about it.

A Great Affirmation

A great affirmation includes the following elements:

- First person [I]
- Present tense [I AM] or [I AM BECOMING]
- Use powerful words that convey pictures or emotions

Examples of Positive Affirmations

- *"I am an unstoppable force!"*
- *"I can, I will, I am going to overcome any obstacle in my way."*
- *"Every 'no' gets me closer to a 'yes.'"*
- *"I'm getting more organized every day."*
- *"If I see more, I sell more."*
- *"It's like me to hit my goals."*
- *"I finish strong because I work the numbers."*
- *"I like pressure; it brings out the best in me."*
- *"If it's going to be, it's up to me."*
- *"Calm and cool, I always deliver."*
- *"Fearless on the phone, 90 minutes of no distractions."*
- *"Every hour gets my best, every person gets my best."*

If you want to take control of your self-talk, the most impactful exercise you can possibly do is to take out a piece of paper and write out a minimum of fifteen positive affirmations. Then, make ten copies of your affirmations and carry them with you, post them on your walls, share them with other people, and, most importantly, say them to yourself out loud every day.

Strategy Tactics

Throughout the book, we mention quite a few tactics and activities that you can do as you head down the road to redefining possible. We want to share them with you here, in one place, to help you best achieve all you want out of life.

These tactics provide practical ways for you to bring the strategies to life. It's important to take the proper time to work through these prompts as you work on redefining possible.

THE TRUE-YOU INTERVIEW

Strategy 2—Ownership

Accountability is making the commitment to improve. This means being open-minded to feedback, especially in areas where you have weaknesses. However, when it comes to ourselves, we have blind spots because we can't see ourselves the way the people closest to us do. You can hold yourself accountable to improving by asking others what they see in you.

The True-You Interview is a system for getting honest feedback. Through asking a series of seven questions to the people who know you best, you can learn about areas in which you might be excelling and other areas where there might be room for improvement.

Pick three to five people in your life that you're fairly close with who would be extremely honest about your strengths and your weaknesses. It could be a significant other, a parent, a best friend, or a coworker. The key is to interview people who will be extremely honest and forthright. You can help by creating a safe environment for them. Tell them that whether it's good or bad, you want to hear it because you're focused on growth and accountability.

THE TRUE-YOU INTERVIEW QUESTIONS:

1. What are my strengths?
2. What do you see as my strengths in my everyday life and business?
3. What are my weaknesses?
4. What doesn't work about the person I am?
5. What do other people count on me for?
6. What do other people know I can't be counted on for?
7. Is there anybody that I should apologize to for wrongdoing?

Being truly accountable means that you have to be vulnerable and totally open to feedback, both positive and negative.

In the space below, list three to five people who are close to you and would give you open and honest feedback to the questions above.

1. _____
2. _____
3. _____
4. _____
5. _____

VISION: YOU ARE IN CONTROL

Strategy 3—Vision

As you thought about your vision and what you would like to be, do, and have in your life, you probably noticed how the world prescribes one way of achieving your goals. The journey to redefining possible is counterintuitive, though.

Most people think that life works like this. . . .

For example:

"If I had more money, then I could do the things I want, and I could be happy."

Successful people understand that life actually works just the opposite. . . .

For example:

"I can be happy, which makes it easy to do the things required so that I can have more money."

20 "WHATS" TO FIND YOUR "WHY"

Strategy 3—Vision

1. What amount of money do you want to make?
2. What places would you like to visit in the world?
3. What type of job would you like to do each day?
4. What would your perfect day look like in terms of how you spent your time and what you were doing?
5. What are the characteristics of your perfect relationship?
6. What do you want to look like?
7. What do you want to give back to the world?
8. What do you want to be known for?
9. What are the things you believe in most?
10. What people can help you get to where you want to go?
11. What are the things you would like to have?
12. What are the most exciting things you'd like to try?
13. What events would you like to go to?
14. What type of house do you want to have?
15. What people would you like to meet?
16. What amount of money do you want to have at retirement?
17. What would you do if you knew you couldn't fail?
18. What things would have to happen in order to accomplish that huge dream?
19. What do you want people to think of when they think of you?
20. What people do you want to spend most of your time with?

15 GOALS TO ACCOMPLISH IN THE NEXT YEAR
Strategy 1—Focus

In this strategy, we discussed the power of writing out your goals on paper. We believe you can accomplish whatever you set out to do! Write out fifteen goals for the year below.

1. _____

2. _____

3. _____

4. _____

5. _____

6. _____

7. _____

8. _____

9. _____

10. _____

11. _____

12. _____

13. _____

14. _____

15. _____

IDENTIFY, DUPLICATE, PERFECT

Strategy 5—Confidence

In strategy five, we discussed how to reach the stage of unconditional confidence as quickly as you can in order to redefine possible. To improve and gain confidence, you can use the Identify, Duplicate, Perfect (IDP) technique, created by Southwestern's Dave Brown, to master your strengths. It's easy to rely on others to give you feedback about what you should be doing better and what you already do well. However, you have the ability to self-evaluate and determine these traits for yourself. No one knows you better than you do.

1. **Identify** the best version of you—what makes you great. At the end of a great week, look back and determine what you did really well. No matter how badly you think you did, there are always a few things that you did right. It can be anything from how you greeted people to how you asked for referrals. What are your strengths? Think of three to four things you already know you do well.

2. **Duplicate** those things you already do well. Come up with a strategy to duplicate each one of those three or four things in every single sales presentation that you do. This allows you to master your optimal habits. Duplicate the version of yourself you bring to the table when you're at the top of your game. Focusing on the strengths you already have helps you build confidence and gives you a positive anchor to rely on in any situation.

3. **Perfect** your strengths by planning to practice. Look at your schedule and decide when you can put your

strengths to use. Proactively planning when to use your strengths will give you confidence in each of those situations.

Focusing on what you do well provides an anchor of confidence that grounds you. For example, going into a sales presentation with the knowledge of what your strengths are can give you the boost of confidence you need to take your presentation to the next level. Incorporate the IDP technique into your schedule next week and notice the difference in your level of confidence.

Identify: _____

_____

_____

_____

Duplicate: _____

_____

_____

_____

Perfect: _____

_____

_____

_____

LITTLE VICTORIES
Strategy 5—Confidence

If you do these ten "little victories" every day, you will have so much positive momentum that your confidence will be at a peak before you even start your workday.

1. Wake up, jump out of bed, and say, "It's going to be a great day!"

2. Hustle to the bathroom, look yourself in the eyes, and say a positive affirmation.

3. Do some kind of physical activity. Work out or do push-ups and sit-ups. Every day, try to do one more repetition than the day before.

4. While getting ready, say ten times, "I can, I will, I'm going to . . . (insert goal for that day)."

5. During breakfast, read something inspirational.

6. After breakfast, take ten minutes to review your "must dos" for the day and visualize success in all of your activities.

7. On your drive to the office, listen to a motivational podcast or audiobook.

8. When you get to work, say something uplifting to the first person you see.

9. Say a positive affirmation out loud before your first phone call, meeting, or presentation.

10. Have your schedule ready and in front of you, and strive to be on time for each event in the day.

Acknowledgments

From Dustin: Thank you, God, for grace, Kyah for love, Haven for joy, Dad and Mom for raising me, Jack and Amy for adopting me, Southwestern for believing and investing in me. Thank you to all of the Southwestern Family of Companies (SWFC) team members for your faith in this mission, vision, and journey we are on together to build SWFC and positively impact the world. Last but certainly not least, thank you, Ron. You have made a huge impact in my life and in the lives of countless others. You inspire me. You are one of my best friends for life. Thank you for who you are and what you stand for. I'm excited to keep redefining possible together!

From Ron: Mom and Dad, you have believed in me through it all—including every boneheaded choice I've ever made. You've always been a shining example for me of God's love and grace. Thank you both. Desireé, you are like no one I've ever met, and I hope this book and I make you proud. I love doing life with you! You are truly my best friend. VPKH, my crazy kids, you make me whole. You three are the biggest reasons behind most of what I do. To our Southwestern family, I have found home and I am grateful.

Twenty-six years so far, and we are just getting started! And to Dustin, you challenge me in every way I think and act . . . and I love being challenged. Thanks for being an authentic friend, a humble leader, and an inspiration to work alongside.

Endnotes

1   Charles Q. Choi, "Human Brain May Be Even More Powerful Computer than Thought," NBC News, October 30, 2013, https://www.nbcnews.com/sciencemain/human-brain-may-be-even-more-powerful-computer-thought-8C11497831.

2   "Dextroamphetamine and Amphetamine," MedlinePlus, accessed March 13, 2020, https://medlineplus.gov/druginfo/meds/a601234.html.

3   Nancy F. Crum-Cianflone et al., "Prescription Stimulants and PTSD Among US Military Service Members," *Journal of Traumatic Stress* 28, no. 6 (December 2015): 585–89, https://doi.org/10.1002/jts.22052.

4   Larry Alton, "Why Clutter Is Killing Your Focus (and How to Fix It)," NBC News, June 22, 2017, https://www.nbcnews.com/better/health/why-clutter-killing-your-focus-how-fix-it-ncna775531.

5   Dr. Henry Cloud and Dr. John Townsend, *Boundaries: When to Say Yes, How to Say No to Take Control of Your Life*, rev. ed. (Grand Rapids, MI: Zondervan, 2017).

6   Ron Breazeale, "Thoughts, Neurotransmitters, Body-Mind Connection," *Psychology Today*, July 17, 2012, https://www.psychologytoday.com/us/blog/in-the-face-adversity/201207/thoughts-neurotransmitters-body-mind-connection.

7   *Merriam-Webster*, s.v. "rationalization," accessed February 14, 2020, https://www.merriam-webster.com/dictionary/rationalization.

8   Malcolm Gladwell, *David and Goliath: Underdogs, Misfits, and the Art of Battling Giants* (New York: Little, Brown and Company, 2013).

9   Christopher N. Cascio et al., "Self-Affirmation Activates Brain Systems Associated with Self-Related Processing and Reward and Is Reinforced by Future Orientation," *Social Cognitive and Affective Neuroscience* 11, no. 4 (November 2015): 621–29, https://doi.org/10.1093/scan/nsv136.

10 Leena Guptha, "To Affirm or Not Affirm?" *Psychology Today*, April 25, 2017, https://www.psychologytoday.com/us/blog/embodied-wellness/201704/affirm-or-not-affirm.

11 Mayo Clinic Staff, "Change Your Mind to Grow," Mayo Clinic, April 24, 2019, https://www.mayoclinic.org/healthy-lifestyle/adult-health/in-depth/change-your-mind-to-grow/art-20342132.

12 "Biography of Nelson Mandela," Nelson Mandela Foundation, accessed April 7, 2020, https://www.nelsonmandela.org/content/page/biography.

13 Eilene Zimmerman, "Survey Shows Visualizing Success Works," *Forbes*, January 27, 2016, https://www.forbes.com/sites/eilenezimmerman/2016/01/27/survey-shows-visualizing-success-works/#7a7adc65760b.

14 Lien B. Pham and Shelley E. Taylor, "From Thought to Action: Effects of Process-Versus Outcome-Based Mental Simulations on Performance," *Personality and Social Psychology Bulletin* 25, no. 2 (February 1999): 250–60, https://doi.org/10.1177/0146167299025002010.

15 Jim Lohr, "Can Visualizing Your Body Doing Something Help You Learn to Do It Better?" *Scientific American*, May 1, 2015, https://www.scientificamerican.com/article/can-visualizing-your-body-doing-something-help-you-learn-to-do-it-better/.

16 *The Last Samurai*, directed by Edward Zwick, written by John Logan, featuring Ken Watanabe and Tom Cruise (Los Angeles: Warner Bros., 2003), DVD.

17 *Merriam-Webster*, s.v. "confidence," accessed February 14, 2020, https://www.merriam-webster.com/dictionary/confidence.

18 "Your Altitude," Ziglar.com, accessed April 17, 2020, https://www.ziglar.com/quotes/your-attitude-not-your-aptitude/.

19 Dr. Henry Cloud and Dr. John Townsend, *Boundaries: When to Say Yes, How to Say No to Take Control of Your Life*, rev. ed. (Grand Rapids, MI: Zondervan, 2017).

20 "Breaking Bad Habits: Why It's So Hard to Change," National Institutes of Health, NIH News in Health, January 2012, accessed June 11, 2020, https://newsinhealth.nih.gov/2012/01/breaking-bad-habits.

21 *Merriam-Webster*, s.v. "faith," accessed February 14, 2020, https://www.merriam-webster.com/dictionary/faith.

22 "Best-Selling Book," Guinness World Records, accessed February 19, 2020, https://www.guinnessworldrecords.com/world-records/best-selling-book-of-non-fiction/.

23 Jeff Goodell, "Steve Jobs in 1994: The Rolling Stone Interview," *Rolling Stone*, January 17, 2011, https://www.rollingstone.com/culture/culture-news/steve-jobs-in-1994-the-rolling-stone-interview-231132/.

24 Mike Berardino, "Mike Tyson Explains One of His Most Famous Quotes," *South Florida SunSentinel*, November 9, 2012, https://www.sun-sentinel.com/

sports/fl-xpm-2012-11-09-sfl-mike-tyson-explains-one-of-his-most-famous-
quotes-20121109-story.html.

25   "Pledge to Eat Less Meat," The Jane Goodall Institute, accessed February 14,
     2020: http://team.janegoodall.org/site/PageServer?pagename=
     ieatmeatless_pledge.

26   Belinda Luscombe, "Do We Need $75,000 a Year to Be Happy?"
     Time, September 6, 2010, http://content.time.com/time/magazine/
     article/0,9171,2019628,00.html.

27   We have found much inspiration in those who found joy in the worst of
     circumstances. Notable Holocaust examples include Elie Wiesel, who wrote
     Night about his experiences in a concentration camp, and Corrie ten Boom,
     whose book *The Hiding Place* chronicled her family's efforts to hide Jewish
     people from the Nazis in her home during World War II. More recently,
     Malala Yousafzai told the story of how she fought for her life in *I Am
     Malala*, and how, against all odds, she found joy in helping young women in
     countries that oppress women's rights.

About the Authors

Ron Alford: As a senior partner, the vice president of recruiting, and an executive-level sales and leadership coach for Southwestern Consulting, Ron Alford is an expert in recruiting, sales training, and coaching, helping individuals and teams to reach higher than they ever imagined. Alford has shattered every sales and revenue record at Southwestern Consulting since joining the company in 2013. He is a company record holder, having personally achieved the highest level of sales seventy times with Southwestern Advantage. He's also a leadership record holder, coaching and training more top 1 percent producers than any other manager since Southwestern Advantage was founded in 1868. Most of all, Alford is a devoted dad and husband, all while continuing to push the distance in his trail-ultrarunning endeavors.

Dustin Hillis: As chief executive officer, Dustin Hillis is leading the vision and strategy to make Southwestern Family of Companies the most impactful privately owned company worldwide. Hillis is also a cofounder of Southwestern Consulting and remains the president of Southwestern Coaching. He is the author of *Navigate: Selling the Way People Like to Buy* and coauthor of

Navigate 2.0 and is an expert in buying, selling, and management psychology and communication styles. While earning his psychology degree as a junior at the University of Tennessee, Hillis broke the all-time sales record for Southwestern Advantage, making a profit of more than $100,000 in fourteen weeks.

Notes

TAKE YOUR SALES TO THE NEXT LEVEL
WITH *NAVIGATE 2.0*!

*Navigate 2.0: Selling the Way People Want
to Buy* by Dustin Hillis and Steve Reiner

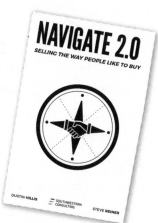

Discover strategies for identifying and
relating to people who have different behavioral profiles, and learn
how to modify your approach and
increase sales.

Book is available separately or as part of the *Navigate 2.0* bundle,
which includes the audiobook, a custom DISC assessment with a
50+ page individualized report, the Navigate module used with
coaching clients, and a 6-part video series.

Visit SouthwesternConsulting.com

Keep the momentum going with these titles, available at SouthwesternConsulting.com:

Performance Under Pressure
By Terry Lyles | Make a permanent shift in your relationship with stress, no matter your circumstances.

Managing for Sales Results
By Ron Marks | Learn how to make the smartest, most profitable hiring decisions for your team.

Gettin' In and Gettin' Out
By Gary Michels | Discover the best way to get in front of decision makers, lead them through the process, and get out with a signed contract.

Southwestern Consulting helps take your business to the next level. We provide 1:1 services for businesses, executives, and thought leaders in addition to online sales training programs for groups and dynamic keynote speakers. If you are interested in coaching or speaking for you or your team, please visit *SouthwesternConsulting.com.*